ONE-MINUTE WEEKLY SPORTS DEVOTIONS FOR RISING ATHLETES

BIBLICAL GUIDANCE FOR TEENS TO PLAY WITH PURPOSE, BUILD MENTAL TOUGHNESS, CRAFT A COMPETITIVE EDGE & LEAD THROUGH CHRIST

NEXTLEVEL PUBLICATIONS

CONTENTS

BONUS: FUEL BEYOND THE PAGES

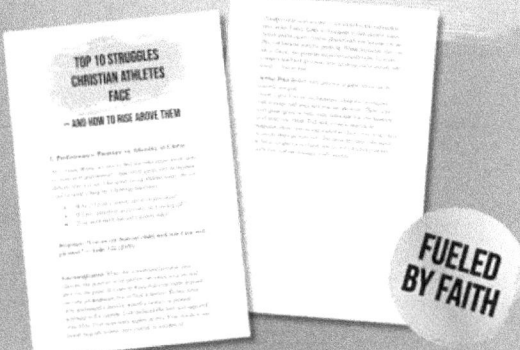

TOP 10 STRUGGLES
... and how to rise above

FUELED
BY FAITH

SCAN ME

WEEKLY GAME PLAN

Every great athlete starts somewhere—just like you. Stephen Curry was once told he was too small to play basketball beyond high school. Katie Ledecky swam laps before dawn while her peers were still asleep. Giannis Antetokounmpo sold trinkets on the streets of Greece before becoming an NBA MVP. What made the difference in their development and rise to the top of their sport? Not just talent, but true grit. Not just hustle, but a humble heart. And above all—an unshakeable faith.

The athletes you admire weren't born into greatness. They trained for it. Their strength didn't come from physical skill alone. It also came from trusting God, staying humble, bouncing back after losses, and leading with purpose. That's what this devotional is about: giving you the spiritual wisdom and strength to grow into the athlete and person God created you to be.

The purpose of this book is to be your weekly faith workout. Just like reps in the gym build muscle, small but steady time in Scripture and prayer will build a foundation of character, discipline, integrity, humility, and spiritual focus that will last far beyond the final scoreboard.

Here's how each weekly devotion is laid out:

- **Victory Verse** —A powerful Scripture that sets the tone and theme for the week.

- **Beyond the Scoreboard**— A short, game-ready lesson featuring real stories from professional Christian athletes and teams who've faced setbacks, stayed faithful, and risen to the top of their sport.

- **Weekly Game Plan**— Reflection questions, a journaling space, and a practical challenge to help you apply the lesson to your sport and your life.

- **The Prayer Zone** —A meaningful, focused prayer to ground your goals in God's truth and realign your heart for the week ahead.

Whether you're starting on the varsity team or just learning the game, *One-Minute Weekly Sports Devotions for Rising Athletes* will equip you with the Biblical guidance you need to play with purpose, build mental toughness, craft a competitive edge, and lead through Christ.

Your sport is a gift, but so is your influence. Use it for good. So, lace up, dig in, and train your heart like you train your body—with passion, purpose, and the power of God's Word.

SECTION 1: FOUNDATIONS OF FAITH

(WEEKS 1 - 14)

This section helps you to anchor your identity in Christ and understand your greater purpose beyond the stats. Before you can lead on the field, you must be anchored in who you are off it. These first devotions equip young athletes with guidance on how to strengthen their identity in Christ, embrace humility and gratitude, and compete with unwavering integrity—laying the spiritual groundwork for a life and game that glorifies God.

CHAPTER 1: PURPOSE & ALL GLORY TO GOD

1

AUDIENCE OF ONE

"Whatever you do, work at it with all your heart, as working for the Lord, not for human masters."
Colossians 3:23

BEYOND THE SCOREBOARD

When NFL linebacker **Shaquille Leonard** entered the league, few believed he'd be a star. He came from a small college and was overlooked in the draft. But Shaq didn't let the negative noise define him. He anchored his confidence in something deeper: his faith in Christ. Shaq didn't play to impress fans or critics—he played for an Audience of One. Every game, he wrote "A.O.1" on his wrist tape to remind himself that his purpose came from God, not the spotlight.

He hustled on every down—not for headlines, but because he knew Who he was playing for—the Lord. He became the NFL Defensive Rookie of the Year, a multi-time All-Pro, and one of the most respected leaders in the league. But his identity stayed rooted in Christ, not in his accomplishments. His mindset reflected the truth of Colossians 3:23, which says that whatever we do, we should give our best effort as if we're doing it for the

Lord, not for the approval of people. It means your effort matters even when no one sees it.

As an athlete, you'll be tempted to perform for popularity, stats, or even social media. But when you remember Who you play for, everything changes. Your practices, your leadership, your attitude on the field—even your failures—all become part of your faith walk through life. When you compete with purpose for the Lord, you're winning in the ways that matter most.

WEEKLY GAME PLAN

Reflection: *In my sport, who do I play for? In what ways do I give my best effort even when no one is looking? Where can I improve?*

Challenge: This week, play like Jesus is in the stands. Whether you're in the zone or having an off day, hustle like it matters to God—because it does. Write "A.O.1" somewhere visible—on your wristband, water bottle, or locker. Live Colossians 3:23 out loud in how you compete, how you treat your teammates, and how you show up on a daily basis—on and off the field.

THE PRAYER ZONE

Dear God, thank You, for the gift of competition and the chance to grow through sports. Help me hustle with purpose and compete with heart. Let my game glorify You, whether I win or lose. Teach me to live for You, God—my true Coach and Champion. **Amen.**

2

SHINE FOR GOD'S GLORY

"Let your light shine before others, that they may see your good deeds and glorify your Father in heaven."
Matthew 5:16

BEYOND THE SCOREBOARD

Softball star **Jennie Finch** wasn't just dominant on the mound—she was a shining light off the field. With Olympic gold medals and a blazing fastball that overwhelmed hitters, Jennie could have made her career all about personal fame. But she didn't. Instead, she used every opportunity to give glory to God. Whether it was praying before games, pointing upward after a win, or speaking publicly about her relationship with Christ, Jennie let the world know who she played for.

She once said, *"My worth is not found in wins. My worth is found in Jesus."* Even as she struck out the best hitters in the world, she remained humble, always redirecting the spotlight to her Savior. She didn't let the spotlight blind her. Instead, she used it to reflect Christ.

That's exactly what Matthew 5:16 is about. Jesus tells us to *"let our light shine"*—not to show off, but to point others to God. When you play with integrity, encourage your teammates, stay calm under pressure, or show kindness to opponents, you're shining God's light.

As a young athlete, your light shines brightest in the little things: how you treat the last player on the bench, how you respond when a call doesn't go your way, and how you carry yourself in wins and losses. You may not have a camera crew at your game, but people are still watching—teammates, opponents, coaches, siblings. Every play is a chance to show what Jesus looks like in action.

WEEKLY GAME PLAN

Reflection: *How can I be a light in my sport? Do my actions lead others closer to Jesus?*

_____

_____

_____

Challenge: Be intentional this week. Smile more and serve more. Encourage teammates who are struggling. Let your good deeds on the field shine—not to make yourself look good, but to reflect Jesus' light and glorify God in every play.

THE PRAYER ZONE

Thank You, Jesus, for the chance to shine Your light through my life and sport. Please help me be a light today. Let my effort, attitude, and words bring You glory. Use my sport as a stage to show others who You are. **Amen.**

3

GIFTED TO GLORIFY

"In all your ways acknowledge Him, and He will make your paths straight."
Proverbs 3:6

BEYOND THE SCOREBOARD

Albert Pujols is one of the greatest hitters in MLB history with over 3,000 hits, 700+ home runs, and multiple MVP awards. But if you asked Albert what mattered most to him, he wouldn't say his stats. He'd say Jesus. From his rookie year to his final season, Pujols used every platform—postgame interviews, charity work, even his retirement speech—to point to God. After hitting his 700th career home run, a reporter asked how it felt. In one of the biggest moments of his career, Albert didn't boast or take credit for his success. Instead, Albert simply said, *"To God be the glory. He's the One who gave me this talent."*

That mindset is straight from Proverbs 3:6. When you acknowledge God in every area of your life, He'll guide your path straight. It reminds us that our talents and successes aren't solely for us—they're meant to glorify God. Albert's success didn't just come from hard work. It came from surrendering everything to the Lord, the good and the struggles. Whether he struck out or hit a walk-off homerun, his focus stayed the same: acknowledging the One who gave him the talent and ability.

Young athletes today have the same opportunity to point back to the Lord and give Him glory. When you give all credit to God, even in a world that chases self-promotion, you will stand out from your peers.

WEEKLY GAME PLAN

Reflection: *Do I take the credit for my talents and successes or give it to God? This week, how can I honor God and give all glory to Him when I win—and when I struggle?*

_____

_____

_____

Challenge: Secretly write Proverbs 3:6 somewhere only you'll see it this week—inside your hat, glove, cleats, or shoes. Remind yourself to acknowledge God out loud when you're complimented and silently thank Him in your heart for your talents every time you take the field or court.

THE PRAYER ZONE

Heavenly Father, thank You for my talents. You're the reason I have these gifts. I don't want the spotlight on me—I want You to shine through me. Help me play with humility and give You credit in everything I do. **Amen.**

4

KINGDOM MINDED ATHLETE

"But seek first his kingdom and his righteousness, and all these things will be given to you as well."
Matthew 6:33

BEYOND THE SCOREBOARD

Stephen Curry has changed the game of basketball. With multiple MVP awards, NBA championships, and a reputation as the greatest shooter in history, he's one of the most recognized athletes in the world. But Steph will tell you: none of it matters more than his relationship with Jesus Christ.

From the start of his career, Steph has made his priorities clear. He points upward after every made shot—not as a celebration of himself, but as a signal of who gets the glory. He writes "I Can Do All Things" on his shoes as a reference to Philippians 4:13. In interviews and award speeches, he consistently praises God. Steph once said, *"I know why I play the game. It's not for stats or popularity. It's to be a witness for Christ."* Curry's story is what it means to be a Kingdom-minded athlete—to live and compete with God's purpose at the center.

Matthew 6:33 teaches us to first seek the Kingdom of God. This means before chasing goals, wins, recognition, or followers, you chase God's will. You follow His ways. You live by His standards. When you do, everything else—confidence, growth, and even opportunities—falls into place in God's timing. On the court, Steph plays to win, but he lives to serve the Lord. As a young athlete, you can follow his example by honoring God with every opportunity.

WEEKLY GAME PLAN

Reflection: *How can I honor Jesus with the stage I currently have?*

_____

_____

_____

Challenge: This week, take a Steph-like approach. Write "Seek First" or "Matthew 6:33" on something you wear for all to see. Before games or practices, pause to ask God for focus and purpose. Compete with excellence but always let your heart aim higher—for Christ's Kingdom, not just a scoreboard.

THE PRAYER ZONE

Thank You, Lord, for giving me gifts I can use for Your Kingdom. Teach me to be a Kingdom-minded athlete—focused not just on winning, but on witnessing for Christ. Like Steph, help me put You first in my mindset, my training, and every moment I compete. Use my game to bring You glory. **Amen.**

CHAPTER 2: HUMILITY & GRATITUDE

5

TEACHABLE & TRUSTING

"He guides the humble in what is right and teaches them his way."
Psalm 25:9

BEYOND THE SCOREBOARD

Jalen Hurts didn't have the smoothest path to NFL greatness. As a young quarterback at Alabama, he led his team to the 2018 national title game—only to be benched at halftime to Tua Tagovailoa. Instead of sulking, complaining, or making it about himself, Jalen responded with humility. He stayed locked in, cheered for his teammate, and finished the season.

The following year, he continued to learn and grow, eventually transferring to Oklahoma, where he had one of the best seasons of his career. He didn't quit. He didn't lash out. He trusted God's path—even when it was hard to understand.

Today, Jalen Hurts is an elite NFL quarterback for the Philadelphia Eagles and a vocal Christian believer. He is well known across the league for his coachability, quiet strength, and unwavering faith. Reporters and coaches constantly praise his teachable spirit, focus, and humility. Psalm 25:9 says that God *"guides the humble"* and *"teaches them His way."* Jalen lives out Psalm 25:9. His growth as a quarterback wasn't just about talent. It was about being humble and having a teachable and trusting heart.

As a young athlete, being teachable isn't just about accepting criticism. It's also about trusting that God can use every setback to grow you athletically and spiritually. Whether you're benched, challenged, or told to try something new, humility invites God to lead you to something better.

WEEKLY GAME PLAN

Reflection: *Where can I be more coachable and humble this week? Do I trust God's plan, even when it's uncomfortable?*

_____

_____

_____

Challenge: This week, focus on being coachable. Ask a coach or teammate one area where you can grow. Don't defend—just listen. Then take it to God in prayer and ask Him to guide your next step. Humility is the gateway to greatness.

THE PRAYER ZONE

Thank You, God, for always leading me with love and wisdom. Keep my heart teachable, even when it's hard to hear correction. Help me trust Your direction more than my own and shape me into the athlete—and person—You've called me to be. **Amen.**

6

VICTORY WITH A HUMBLE HEART

"He has shown you, O mortal, what is good. And what does the Lord require of you? To act justly and to love mercy and to walk humbly with your God."
Micah 6:8

BEYOND THE SCOREBOARD

Kyle Snyder is one of the most dominant American wrestlers of all time. At just 20 years old, he became the youngest American to win Olympic gold in wrestling. He's also won multiple world championships and NCAA titles. But if you listen to Kyle talk, you won't hear pride or arrogance. Instead, you'll hear humility—and faith.

In interviews, Kyle often points to his relationship with Christ as his foundation. He's said, *"The most important thing in my life is my faith. That's what gives me peace, not wrestling."* Even after winning some of the world's biggest matches, Kyle keeps his focus on growing in his faith and path with God—not chasing medals. He also honors his opponents, thanks his coaches, and rarely talks about his own dominance. His attitude strongly reflects Micah 6:8, which tells us that God calls us to act with integrity, show kindness, and walk humbly with Him. That doesn't mean holding back in competitions—it means competing with character.

Kyle trains and wrestles with full intensity, but he doesn't let ego take the mat. For young athletes, this is the perfect model: give 100% effort but stay grounded. Hustle hard but walk humbly. Let your humility and humble character speak louder than your stats.

WEEKLY GAME PLAN

Reflection: *Do I compete with humility and kindness? How do I treat teammates and opponents when I win or lose? What part of Micah 6:8 can I live out more this week?*

_____

_____

_____

Challenge: This week, take the message of Micah 6:8 into your sport. Work hard, stay kind, and keep your head down—even when you shine. Let your game glorify God, not your ego.

THE PRAYER ZONE

Thank You, Lord, for the opportunity to compete, grow, and glorify You through my sport. Help me live out Micah 6:8 by competing hard, staying humble, and reflecting Your character in how I lead my teammates and how I play. **Amen.**

7

GRATEFUL THROUGH THE STORM

"Give thanks to the Lord, for he is good; his love endures forever."
Psalm 107:1

BEYOND THE SCOREBOARD

Bethany Hamilton is a professional surfer best known for her inspiring comeback after surviving a shark attack at age 13. On October 31, 2003, Bethany was attacked by a 14-foot tiger shark while surfing off the coast of Hawaii. She lost her left arm and over 60% of her blood. Her survival was considered a miracle—but what stunned the world was her return to surfing just one month later. Despite the odds, Bethany relearned how to surf with one arm, returned to competition just two years later, and has earned top finishes in World Surf League events, proving her elite skill.

What fueled her comeback was her unwavering faith and gratitude. In interviews, Hamilton regularly says, *"I might not have two arms, but I have a thankful heart, and I know God can still use me. God gave me this story for a reason."*

Bethany has said her strength and purpose come entirely from her faith in Christ. She speaks at churches and Christian conferences, sharing how she's grateful not for the loss, but for what God has done through the pain. She thanks God for what she *can* do instead of focusing on what she lost.

Psalm 107:1 reminds us that God's goodness and love are constant—even when life gets hard. Gratitude in the storm doesn't mean you ignore the struggles—it means you choose to praise God through it and trust the story He has planned out for you. Bethany's story teaches us that setbacks don't define you—your response does. As a young athlete, there will be losses, injuries, and seasons that feel unfair. Like Bethany, you can say, *"Thank You, Lord, I trust You,"* even in the middle of challenging moments.

WEEKLY GAME PLAN

Reflection: *How can I show gratitude in hard times?*

_____

_____

_____

Challenge: Think of a tough situation you're facing—injury, pressure, failure. Write a short prayer of gratitude for what God is teaching you through it.

THE PRAYER ZONE

Lord, thank You for Your goodness, even in the hard times. Teach me to praise You in the storm and give me a thankful heart, full of faith and trust. **Amen.**

8

KINGDOM OVER CLOUT

"Do nothing out of selfish ambition or vain conceit. Rather, in humility, value others above yourselves."
Philippians 2:3

BEYOND THE SCOREBOARD

When **Mallory Pugh Swanson** joined the U.S. Women's National Soccer Team as a teen and was instantly thrown into the spotlight, she had every reason to chase fame. She was one of the youngest rising stars in the sport. But instead of seeking clout, she remained humble and kept her heart grounded in Christ.

She's openly shared that her faith helps her stay humble and focused, even when the world praises her. Whether scoring goals or riding the bench, she consistently puts her team first and avoids the pride trap. As a Kingdom-minded athlete, Mallory knows that true greatness is found in serving others, not flexing for the crowd.

Philippians 2:3 calls us away from selfish ambition—toward valuing others above ourselves. Mallory's story shows us what that looks like in action:

celebrating teammates, submitting to coaches, and trusting God more than chasing accolades. She models that true greatness is found not in clout, but in Christ-centered humility and gratefulness.

God calls us to value our teammates, coaches, and even opponents above ourselves. You may not be on a global stage like Mallory, but you face the same choice: chase clout or choose the Kingdom. For young athletes like yourself, this means choosing teamwork over spotlight, relying on faith rather than fame, and embracing setbacks as opportunities to grow in Christ-like character.

WEEKLY GAME PLAN

Reflection: *Do I use my platform to lift myself up or others? How can I put teammates and coaches above myself this week?*

_____

_____

_____

Challenge: In your next game or practice, pick one moment to honor someone else—pass the ball, praise a teammate, or thank a coach. Choose humility over hype. Kingdom over clout.

THE PRAYER ZONE

Thank You, Jesus, for giving me a stage to reflect Your goodness and love. Teach me to put others before myself and to live for Your Kingdom, not for applause. Give me a humble heart, like Mallory's, that trusts You more than the spotlight. **Amen.**

9

CROWNED WITH HUMILITY

"Clothe yourselves with humility... for God opposes the proud but gives grace to the humble."

1 Peter 5:5

BEYOND THE SCOREBOARD

In 2022, the **Georgia Bulldogs** made history—winning back-to-back College Football National Championships with a 15-0 season. They crushed TCU 65-7 in the final game. But what impressed many wasn't just the scoreboard—it was their posture.

Head Coach Kirby Smart and quarterback Stetson Bennett didn't use their big moment to brag. Instead, they praised their teammates, honored their opponents, and gave thanks to God for the opportunity. More than once, Coach Smart referenced their team's faith and the importance of staying hungry and humble. The team celebrated big—but not with arrogance.

That's what 1 Peter 5:5 teaches us: true greatness isn't loud or self-centered. It's clothed in humility and gratitude. It doesn't have to shout because it knows where the strength came from. Humble athletes don't downplay their success—they keep their egos in check. Georgia's players trained like champions, played like warriors, and celebrated like men who hadn't forgotten where they came from. That's the kind of legacy that goes beyond a trophy—it reflects character.

As a young athlete, you have the same opportunity to win with humility and gratitude. Give God the glory. Honor your coaches, teammates, and opponents. Stay grounded. That's what greatness really looks like.

WEEKLY GAME PLAN

Reflection: *Do I stay grounded after big wins? How can I give credit without stealing it for myself? In what ways can I be humble and grateful this week?*

Challenge: Next time you win or succeed, flip the script—brag on a teammate, thank a coach, or recognize someone who helped you get there. Let your humility be louder than your highlight.

THE PRAYER ZONE

Heavenly Father, thank You for the opportunities to excel that You've laid out before me. Please help me stay humble in the high moments. Let success never go to my head. Teach me to use my victories as opportunities to show humility and gratitude and reflect Your grace. **Amen.**

CHAPTER 3: INTEGRITY & RESPECT

10

CHARACTER BEATS STATS

"But seek first his kingdom and his righteousness, and all these things will be given to you as well."
Proverbs 22:1

BEYOND THE SCOREBOARD

Giannis Antetokounmpo has it all—NBA championships, MVP awards, scoring records, and worldwide fame. However, the thing that makes him stand out isn't on a stat sheet—it's his Christ-like character, humility, gratitude, and integrity.

Giannis grew up in poverty with almost nothing. His family, immigrants from Nigeria, struggled to survive in Greece. That background could've made him hardened, but instead, it formed in him deep gratitude and perspective. Despite fame and wealth, Giannis is known for simple living, giving back, and putting his team above personal stats. Giannis has said, *"I always thank God for putting me in this position... It's all by His grace."* His humility is not a PR move—it's who he is. Giannis consistently credits his teammates after big wins, plays selflessly, encourages rookies, owns up to mistakes, and never brags. He doesn't let success go to his head. That's

Christ-like character: putting others first, walking humbly, and always pointing back to God.

Proverbs 22:1 reminds us that a good name—your reputation, integrity, and witness—is more valuable than riches or fame. Giannis reflects that truth. He shows young athletes that who you are matters more than what you accomplish. Stats will fade. Records get broken. But the way you treat people and the integrity you bring to your sport will echo far longer than your stats. If you want to be great in God's eyes, build your character like Giannis. Be honest. Stay thankful. Treat others with respect. Praise your teammates. Let your name reflect Jesus.

WEEKLY GAME PLAN

Reflection: *Am I building a name that reflects Jesus? Do my actions match the values I say I believe?*

Challenge: This week, choose character over attention. Serve someone quietly. Own up to a mistake. Play selflessly. Encourage someone else's success. Let your name be one that honors Christ.

THE PRAYER ZONE

Thank You, Lord, for shaping my heart and reminding me that who I am matters more than what I achieve. God, help me build a name that reflects Your heart. Teach me to lead with humility and live with integrity, just like Giannis. Let others see You through how I compete. **Amen.**

11

TRAIN WITH INTEGRITY

"Whoever walks in integrity walks securely, but whoever takes crooked paths will be found out."
Proverbs 10:9

BEYOND THE SCOREBOARD

Sydney McLaughlin-Levrone is one of the most dominant track athletes of her generation—holding multiple world records in the 400m hurdles and earning back-to-back Olympic gold medals in Tokyo 2020 and Paris 2024. But beyond her speed, Sydney is known for who she is off the track, rooted in her vibrant Christian faith. She has said, *"I'm a child of God... that sets me free to run the race God has set out for me."* Sydney follows Christ and invites Him into everything she does, especially her training.

For Sydney, training with integrity means letting her faith shape her character in every mile and inviting God into the process. She prays before races—with her coach, trainer, and husband—centering her focus not on medals but on glorifying God. Sydney regularly prays before training sessions, asking the Holy Spirit to guide her focus and attitude. She is highly disciplined and honest in her training and preparation, even when no one's watching. She always gives her best, and her work ethic is consistent, because it honors God. Sydney is a model of integrity by respecting and honoring others. She treats coaches, teammates, and even rivals with humility and respect, reflecting Christ in how she competes.

Proverbs 10:9 reminds us that those who walk in integrity walk with security and peace. For young athletes, this means showing up early, staying honest in your reps, and competing in a way that reflects Jesus—on and off the field. You can learn from Sydney's example: train honestly, be consistent, and put God first—even when no one's watching. Let your integrity guide your workouts, how you treat teammates, and how you handle both wins and tough days.

WEEKLY GAME PLAN

Reflection: *Am I honest in my training—even when it's hard? How can I let my faith guide my daily practices this week?*

Challenge: Begin each practice this week with a brief prayer. Be intentional in your daily training; stay consistent, give your best, and honor God by competing with integrity.

THE PRAYER ZONE

Dear Lord, thank You, for allowing me to train, grow, and honor You with how I compete. Help me train like Sydney—with integrity, discipline, humility, and faith. Teach me to walk securely in You, not seeking praise, but seeking to honor Your Name. **Amen.**

12

RESPECT ALL, FEAR NONE

"Be strong and courageous. Do not be afraid; do not be discouraged, for the Lord your God will be with you wherever you go."
Joshua 1:9

BEYOND THE SCOREBOARD

Caeleb Dressel, a decorated Olympic swimmer, blazed onto the international scene at the 2016 Rio Olympics, winning two gold medals as a fresh-faced teenager. Since then, he's cemented his legacy with multiple world records and seven gold medals at Tokyo 2020. Beyond his impressive stats, it's his heart posture that defines him—a genuine mix of respect for the competition and a fearless trust in Jesus.

Dressel often starts his races with quiet prayer, acknowledging that God—not the crowd, nor the records—is the source of his strength. He respects every swimmer in the lane beside him. He never underestimates his opponents, but he doesn't fear them either. If you pay close attention, you will notice that in press conferences, he never puts down other swimmers; instead, he celebrates their achievements, saying things like, *"They earned this. I came to compete with respect."*

Joshua 1:9 reminds us to be strong and courageous, not because of our power, but because God is with us. Caeleb embodies that truth: he competes hard but with an unshakeable confidence rooted in Christ. He doesn't let pressure or rivals shake his peace—because his identity isn't in medals, it's in his Savior.

Young athletes can follow Dressel's lead: respect the opponent, respect the process, and respect your coaches—but never fear because God goes before you. When you step on the field, court, or pool knowing Jesus is by your side to guide you, you're free to compete boldly and honorably.

WEEKLY GAME PLAN

Reflection: *Do I respect my opponents even when I'm intimidated? What fears are holding me back?*

_____

_____

_____

Challenge: In your next competition, pick a moment to pray—either before or after—and ask God for courage and respect in that game. Speak a word of encouragement to an opponent or teammate. Let your confidence display God's presence, not just your ability.

THE PRAYER ZONE

My Lord and Savior, thank You for the strength to compete with courage and grace. Help me respect every competitor and never fear the challenge. Use my boldness to show Your power and point others to You. **Amen.**

13

REVERENCE IN EVERY REP

"And whatever you do, whether in word or deed, do it all in the name of the Lord Jesus, giving thanks to God the Father through him."
Colossians 3:17

BEYOND THE SCOREBOARD

With seven Olympic medals and 25 World Championship golds, **Simone Biles** is widely regarded as the greatest gymnast of all time. What sets her at the top of her game? It's how she trains and competes—with reverence, discipline, and faith. She acknowledges her abilities are a gift from God, and she doesn't perform to impress the crowd. Instead, she competes to honor her Creator.

In training, Simone is known for being meticulous, focused, and fully present. She listens, encourages others, and honors the hard work behind every small detail. She prays before events, thanks God after each meet, and has never lost sight of where her talent came from. At the 2021 Tokyo Olympics, Simone made headlines when she withdrew from multiple events to protect her mental health. This was hard for the world to understand. But behind that bold move was something more profound: a reverence for what God values most—her soul over her score. She reminded the world, *"God is bigger than gymnastics."*

Reverence means showing deep respect, awe, and honor—especially toward God. Colossians 3:17 reminds us that every word and deed should be done in Jesus' name, with gratitude and reverence. That includes training reps, warm-ups, stretches, and big performances. It's showing up with focus and giving your best—to worship God. Simone teaches young athletes that true greatness doesn't come from medals, but from doing every rep with integrity, thankfulness, and reverence for the One who gave you the talent. Reverence is a mindset that can shape your practice, your sportsmanship, and your attitude.

WEEKLY GAME PLAN

Reflection: *Do I train with gratitude, focus, and reverence, or just to "get through it"? How can I treat every rep like an act of worship?*

_____

_____

_____

Challenge: This week, show reverence in how you prepare. Don't just go through the motions. Be fully present in warm-ups and pray before drills. Train like your effort is an offering to God.

THE PRAYER ZONE

Dear God, thank You for the gifts You've given me. Help me show reverence in every rep and treat each moment as worship. Let my words, effort, and attitude reflect Your name. **Amen.**

SECTION II: DISCIPLINE & PERSONAL GROWTH

(WEEKS 14 - 30)

Greatness isn't given—it's forged through daily discipline, mental grit, and faith-fueled perseverance. This set of devotions equips young athletes to embrace the grind—developing habits of discipline, patience, and mental toughness that fuel long-term success. Through stories of resilience and training with purpose, you will learn how to push through adversity with a Christ-centered mindset. These devotions will help you grow not just in skill, but in character, focus, and spiritual maturity.

CHAPTER 4: DISCIPLINE & TRAINING

14

HONORING GOD WITH YOUR HABITS

"Therefore, I urge you, brothers and sisters, in view of God's mercy, to offer your bodies as a living sacrifice, holy and pleasing to God—this is your true and proper worship."

Romans 12:1

BEYOND THE SCOREBOARD

For MLB star **Mookie Betts**, baseball is more than just a profession—it's a platform of worship. He's known for his elite athletic ability and for the intentional way he disciplines himself, both physically and spiritually, to honor God. Mookie's approach to training is intense. In the offseason and during playoff slumps, he's been known to wake up before dawn for solo sessions, taking hundreds of swings at 4:30 a.m., fine-tuning his timing and form. That level of discipline is a reflection of a heart surrendered to the process God has called him to steward. When he lost weight to prevent injuries, Mookie restructured his diet and lifestyle with a mindset of purpose over comfort. That's Romans 12:1 in action: offering his body as a living sacrifice to God and his sport.

Beyond the field, Mookie gives public glory to God. On social media, he consistently posts thanks to the Lord, never shying away from crediting his success to God's mercy. His integrity, servant leadership, and quiet confidence all point back to a man striving to honor Christ in his daily choices.

Romans 12:1 reminds us that our bodies, training, attitudes, and actions are all acts of worship. Just like sticking to your workouts, discipline in your spiritual habits also means choosing God's ways daily through honesty, kindness, and hard work. It's saying "no" to shortcuts and pride, and "yes" to discipline, humility, and integrity—even when it's hard.

WEEKLY GAME PLAN

Reflection: *Where do I need more discipline in my sport and obedience in my faith?*

_____

_____

_____

Challenge: This week, treat your sport like a form of worship. Wake up early to stretch, eat with intention, and train with extra effort. Write Romans12:1 on your wristband to remind yourself to honor God, physically and spiritually.

THE PRAYER ZONE

Thank You, God, for the opportunity to train and compete in my sport. Help me honor You with my training, my daily choices, and my discipline. Teach me to say "no" to shortcuts and pride, and "yes" to discipline and Your ways. **Amen.**

15

DISCIPLINE DRIVES GREATNESS

"No discipline seems pleasant at the time, but painful. Later on, however, it produces a harvest of righteousness and peace for those who have been trained by it."

Hebrews 12:11

BEYOND THE SCOREBOARD

Jordan Morris knows the grind of discipline better than most professional athletes. A standout forward for the Seattle Sounders FC and the U.S. Men's National Soccer Team, Jordan has faced more than his fair share of setbacks—two ACL tears, a major hamstring injury, and daily challenges of managing Type 1 diabetes. Instead of quitting, Jordan leaned into painful discipline—not just in physical therapy, but in trusting God through the process. He trained when he didn't feel like it and stuck to routines when results were slow. He found peace not in quick comebacks, but in quiet faith. That kind of mindset doesn't happen overnight. It's built in the unseen hours, in painful workouts, lonely rehab sessions, and devotionals like this that fuel both the body and spirit.

The same goes for discipline in worship. With school, practice, and life pulling you in every direction, it's easy to forget about spending time with God. Just as exercise and strength training make you stronger physically, praying and reading the Bible build your spiritual strength. Even a few minutes of Scripture each day helps grow your faith and keeps you focused. Hebrews 12:11 doesn't sugarcoat it—discipline is hard. It stretches us, humbles us, and often hurts. But it also produces a bountiful harvest of peace, righteousness, and strength. Greatness doesn't come from hype. It comes from discipline, physically and spiritually, from showing up, pressing through, and worshiping God even on the hard days.

WEEKLY GAME PLAN

Reflection: *Where do I need to push through discomfort in my training? How can I incorporate worship and Scripture into my daily discipline?*

_____

_____

_____

Challenge: Choose two things from your routine—one physical, one spiritual—and give it your complete discipline. Trust God with the harvest that will soon follow.

THE PRAYER ZONE

Thank You, Lord, for the strength and discipline You've given me to grow through every challenge. Discipline is hard, but I know You use it to develop me spiritually and physically. Please help me to stay faithful to the process even when it's tough. Shape me into the athlete and person You've called me to be. **Amen.**

16

FAITH-FUELED OBEDIENCE

"Walk in obedience to all that the Lord your God has commanded you, so that you may live and prosper and prolong your days in the land that you will possess."
Deuteronomy 5:33

BEYOND THE SCOREBOARD

Tony Finau is one of the most admired professional golfers for his smooth swing and powerful drive, but most importantly for the way he lives out his faith. While many athletes focus only on performance, Tony walks in obedience to God's command.

Regarding golf, Tony shows obedience through his disciplined training and steady routines. Golf requires relentless repetition, patience, and mental toughness—and Tony never cuts corners. He trains hard, stays grounded, and honors God through quiet consistency. Even in trials—like his painful ankle injury at the 2018 Masters—Tony didn't panic or give up. He stayed calm, prayed, trusted God, and competed with courage. He trusted that God's plan was greater than the setback. Spiritually, Tony starts each round of golf in prayer, not asking to win, but thanking God for the opportunity. *"I think I have a grateful heart,"* he says. *"I want to make sure God knows that."* His attitude shows that obedience starts with humility and trust, not pride or self-promotion. He always keeps God first.

Tony's life reflects the truth in Deuteronomy 5:33: when we obey God fully, He directs our steps, blesses our journey, and gives us a lasting impact. That's what Deuteronomy 5:33 is all about—walking with God in every detail, not just in the spotlight. Young athletes can learn from Tony: God isn't impressed by how "sacrificial" we look or the numbers on the scoreboard. He's moved by our obedience and willingness to follow His lead every day.

WEEKLY GAME PLAN

Reflection: *Am I more focused on looking "spiritual" or actually obeying God? Where in my training or life do I need to listen to God and obey more fully?*

_____

_____

_____

Challenge: This week, practice silent obedience. Whether it's reading Scripture or faithfully sticking to your workouts, do it to honor Him. Ask God to guide you, and obey what He shows you, even if it's hard.

THE PRAYER ZONE

Thank You, God, for guiding my steps and giving me the faith to follow Your lead. Help me walk in obedience to You. Teach me to walk with You daily, not just when it's easy or visible, but in every moment. Make my training a way to honor You, every step of the way. **Amen.**

17

POWERED BY PRAYER

"Devote yourselves to prayer, being watchful and thankful."
Colossians 4:2

BEYOND THE SCOREBOARD

Before the first whistle blows or the scoreboard lights up, the **Baylor University women's volleyball team** is already winning—on their knees. This nationally ranked team has built a culture where their faithful discipline of team prayer is just as important as practice, and honoring God is the foundation of their game. Each game, win or lose, they join in a prayer circle on the court—praying for God's guidance, thanking Him for the opportunity to compete, and even praying over their opponents. Their pre-game prayers aren't just tradition—they're discipline. They set aside time even in a packed schedule to invite God into their competition, demonstrating reverence and humility in the middle of pressure and performance. Freshman Kendal Murphy shared, *"Putting God at the center of everything... remembering who we're playing for."* Not only does the team pray before the match, but they also pray afterward—regardless of the outcome. They'll extend grace and blessing to their opponents, showing that their mission goes beyond volleyball: it's about pointing others to Christ.

Colossians 4:2 urges us to *"be devoted to prayer, being watchful and thankful."* The Baylor team models this by consistently praying through every serve and set, maintaining spiritual focus in the midst of the sport. It's more than a ritual to the team—it's their power source. For young athletes, this reminds us that prayer isn't just for before bed. It can fuel your performance, calm your nerves, and keep your heart centered. When you discipline yourself to pray intentionally, you're unlocking a strength beyond what your body can produce.

WEEKLY GAME PLAN

Reflection: *Do I make prayer a regular part of my prep—before practices, big games, or only when the pressure hits? What difference does praying with your team make in your heart?*

_____

_____

_____

Challenge: Before your next practice or game, gather with your teammates to pray, even if it's for 30 seconds. Thank God for the opportunity, ask Him to guide your hearts, and pray for your opponents.

THE PRAYER ZONE

Heavenly Father, thank You for this gift of sport. Help me lean on You through prayer—before, during, and after I compete. Give me the discipline of prayer to stay connected to You and the power to fuel my performance. **Amen.**

SUPPORT THE MISSION

At NextLevel Publications, we're passionate about creating meaningful resources that help athletes grow—not just in their sport, but in their walk with Christ. Every story, scripture, challenge, and prayer was thoughtfully chosen to show how your game and faith can work together to shape who you're becoming.

If this devotional has encouraged you or helped you grow spiritually so far, we'd love to hear which devotion(s) have impacted you the most. Leaving a short review not only supports our faith-based mission, but also helps other athletes and families discover a book that could impact their lives too.

Thanks for being part of God's team! Let your voice encourage the next athlete rising up in faith. Please scan the QR code below to leave a review. It only takes a few seconds, and we'd greatly appreciate it!

CHAPTER 5: PATIENCE & PERSEVERANCE

18

PATIENCE BRINGS PROGRESS

"Let perseverance finish its work so that you may be mature and complete, not lacking anything."
James 1:4

BEYOND THE SCOREBOARD

In a world that celebrates instant wins and viral success, patience can feel like a weakness—but in truth, it's one of the strongest qualities an athlete can build. Patience is not passive waiting; it's active trust in God's timing, even when results take time. Few athletes model this better than **Coco Gauff**, the rising tennis star who burst onto the scene at just 15, but has grown stronger with time. Coco had the talent early, but instead of getting caught up in the pressure and fame, she stayed patient in her development. She trusted the process of progress and stayed faithful to her calling. She endured early losses, intense competition, and media hype without skipping the steps of growth. In 2023, her patience paid off when she won her first Grand Slam title at the U.S. Open at just 19 years old.

What's even more inspiring is her heart. In interviews, Coco thanks God before anyone else and is often seen praying before matches. Her quiet confidence and humility model a young athlete deeply rooted in faith. She once said, *"I just put my trust in God and know everything happens for a reason."*

Young athletes today are pushed to rush, to compare, to be recruited at higher levels, and to post the perfect highlight on social media. Patience reminds us that God grows greatness one practice, one prayer, and one moment at a time. Trust the process, and the progress will come.

WEEKLY GAME PLAN

Reflection: *Where in my sport do I struggle with patience the most? In what specific ways can I trust God's timing in my athletic journey?*

_____

_____

_____

Challenge: Remind yourself that real growth takes time. Don't rush what God is shaping in you. Whether it's your skill, your leadership, or your mindset, stay committed to the reps and routines. Be patient with your progress and persistent in your purpose. Write this on your water bottle: *"Patience = Progress."* Let it fuel your focus every day this week.

THE PRAYER ZONE

Dear Jesus, thank You for reminding me that growth takes time and that You are working on me even in the waiting. Help me stay patient when things feel slow or frustrating. Teach me to trust You in the small steps and steady progress. **Amen.**

19

FAITH MOVES MOUNTAINS

"Truly I tell you, if you have faith as small as a mustard seed... nothing will be impossible for you."
Matthew 17:20

BEYOND THE SCOREBOARD

Faith isn't about having everything figured out—it's about trusting God when everything feels uncertain, and nothing is going your way. Few athletes know this better than **Scott Hamilton**, one of the greatest figure skaters of all time. From childhood illness that stunted his growth, to multiple battles with cancer and brain tumors, Scott's journey was never smooth. However, through it all, his faith in Jesus gave him the strength to keep going and to keep skating. After winning Olympic gold in 1984, Scott didn't just change figure skating with his signature moves—he changed lives with his testimony. He often says, *"Faith gives you the courage to endure. The only thing that got me through the darkest seasons of my life was knowing God had a plan—even when I couldn't see it."* Scott's attitude in life was rooted in God. Scott turned his trials and setbacks into a stage, inspiring millions with his perseverance and bold faith in Christ.

Matthew 17:20 tells us that even a tiny seed of faith can move mountains—not always by removing the obstacle, but by giving us the strength to overcome it. When you feel like giving up or you're not getting the results you want, remember that God works in the waiting, and his timing is always perfect. Stay faithful. Keep training and showing up because faith and perseverance are the most powerful combo in your playbook.

WEEKLY GAME PLAN

Reflection: *What "mountain" or struggle am I facing right now in my sport or life? Do I trust that God can use it for His purpose—even if I don't understand it yet?*

_____

_____

_____

Challenge: This week, write *"Faith Moves Mountains"* on your mirror or locker. When doubt creeps in, say a short prayer: *"God, I trust You with this moment."* Keep practicing, competing, and living like God is already working on your story. Show up with courage, knowing God is bigger than anything standing in your way.

THE PRAYER ZONE

Thank You, God, for the strength that comes through faith and the hope You give me to overcome every obstacle. Please give me the faith to keep going when it's hard. Help me trust You with the "mountains" or barriers that are in front of me and make me strong, not just in performance, but in faith and perseverance. **Amen.**

20

TESTED, TOUGH, & TRIUMPHANT

"But he knows the way that I take; when he has tested me, I will come forth as gold."
Job 23:10

BEYOND THE SCOREBOARD

Everyone loves a victory. But what about when you're benched, broken, or forgotten? For **Klay Thompson**, one of the NBA's most clutch shooters and a 4x NBA champion with the Golden State Warriors, the test came hard. In 2019, Klay tore his ACL in the NBA Finals. While rehabbing, he ruptured his Achilles tendon, forcing him out of basketball for 941 days. Two years of silence, setbacks, and suffering. Most thought he was done. But Klay never gave in or let the doubt define him. He stayed locked in, working behind the scenes, rehabbing for nearly 2.5 years. He stayed tough and leaned on the support of his faith, quietly working through the pain and isolation. He shared, *"I leaned on prayer. That got me through. I trusted that God had something better on the other side."*

God had big plans for Klay. In 2022, Klay returned to the court and helped lead the Warriors to another NBA title. He returned with a deeper gratitude, patience, and love for the game. The guy who was nearly forgotten became a champion once again—triumphant, tested, and tougher than ever.

Job 23:10 says when we're tested, we come out like gold. God doesn't waste our trials. He uses them to refine us and prepare us for something greater. Young athlete, like gold in fire, tough moments forge stronger faith. You might face your own injury, doubt, or delay—but don't let the fire break you. Stay faithful in the unseen hours and push through the rehab, the rejection, and the hard practices. God will shape your trials into triumph.

WEEKLY GAME PLAN

Reflection: *What is one challenge I'm currently facing in my sport, training, or mindset? How might God be using that challenge to refine me?*

_____

_____

_____

Challenge: This week, identify a "fire moment"—a challenging workout, a frustrating loss, or a moment of doubt—and choose faith over frustration. When it gets hard, remind yourself: "This moment is forging something greater in me."

THE PRAYER ZONE

Heavenly Father, thank You for staying with me through every trial. When I feel tested, remind me that You are with me in the fire. Refine my faith and use every challenge to prepare me for something greater. **Amen.**

21

PERSEVERE FOR THE PROMISE

"You need to persevere so that when you have done the will of God, you will receive what he has promised."
Hebrews 10:36

BEYOND THE SCOREBOARD

When the odds are stacked against you, perseverance becomes a choice. Will you give up—or keep pushing toward the promise? Perseverance isn't just about endurance—it's about obedience in the waiting. It's trusting that what God has in store is worth the patience, the preparation, and the pressure. **Erin Jackson** knows what that looks like. A standout in-line skater and roller derby athlete, she didn't lace up her first pair of speed skates until 2016. Just months later, she made the U.S. Olympic team—but in the 2018 Olympics, she finished near the bottom. Critics doubted she'd be back. Erin didn't listen to the doubters. She trained in the shadows, trusted the process, and did the quiet work no one sees. Then in 2022, her Olympic dreams nearly slipped away after a stumble in the trials. But, in an incredible act of sportsmanship, teammate Brittany Bowe gave up her own spot to let Erin race. Erin didn't waste the opportunity. She made history by winning Olympic gold in the 500m, becoming the first Black woman to medal in speed skating.

Her journey echoes Hebrews 10:36: she persevered, walked in God's will, and received the promise. This Scripture emphasizes that God honors perseverance that is rooted in trust and obedient to His timing. As a young athlete, your promise might feel far off. But God sees your discipline. He honors your commitment. When you stay faithful and keep showing up with perseverance, He brings the breakthrough in His perfect time. Don't rush the promise. Persevere until it's yours.

WEEKLY GAME PLAN

Reflection: *What area of your sport or life are you being called to stay faithful in—even when the results haven't come yet?*

_____

_____

_____

Challenge: Choose one area in your sport where you've been tempted to give up. Pair every training session with a short prayer asking God to strengthen your perseverance and remind you of the promise ahead.

THE PRAYER ZONE

Thank you, Lord, for the strength to keep going when the journey gets tough. When progress feels slow and the promise feels far away, please help me stay faithful. Remind me that You are constantly working on me, even in the waiting. Give me the grit to persevere and the heart to trust that what You've started in me, You will finish. **Amen.**

22

TRUST, THE HARVEST WILL COME

"Let us not become weary in doing good, for at the proper time we will reap a harvest if we do not give up."
Galatians 6:9

BEYOND THE SCOREBOARD

Trusting the promise means believing in what you can't yet see. Few athletes have exemplified this better than **Carli Lloyd**, an American professional soccer player, whose career is defined by relentless perseverance and faith in God's timing. After winning gold at the 2008 Olympics, Carli faced knee injuries and a season of underperformance. But she trusted God and had faith in the process—committing to rehab, showing up to extra training, and placing her hope in more than her own ability. Her harvest came in breathtaking fashion: during the 2015 Women's World Cup final, Carli scored a "hat trick"—two from midfield—and earned Player of the Match honors. That game didn't just win the World Cup—it stood as the harvest of years spent training in the shadows, trusting each rep and each prayer. Carli openly credits her faith, saying *"I believe God is in control* *of everything..."* when asked about her performance under pressure. Her humility, focus, and intentional work show that even champions need seasons of trials, quiet faith, and trust before they shine.

In Carli's story, Galatians 6:9 unfolds in real life. She didn't sprint to success. She persevered, trusted God through the setbacks, and reaped the harvest God had prepared for her. As a young athlete, it's important to understand that your harvest might not come today or even tomorrow. Still, it's already growing in the unseen moments. Keep pushing, keep praying, and trust God's promise—your harvest is on the horizon.

WEEKLY GAME PLAN

Reflection: *What "unseen" work in your sport or faith journey feels tiring right now? How can you shift your mindset to trust that the harvest is coming?*

_____

_____

_____

Challenge: Write down one goal you've been working toward in your sport that you aren't seeing the results as quickly as hoped for. Underneath it, list 3 ways you can stay faithful and committed—especially when it's hard.

THE PRAYER ZONE

Thank You, Lord, for reminding me that the seeds I plant in faith are never wasted. Help me stay faithful even when results don't come quickly. Teach me to trust Your timing and help me see that the harvest is already growing—one rep, one prayer, one day at a time. **Amen.**

CHAPTER 6: RESILIENCE & RECOVERY

23

BOUNCE BACK BELIEF

"Though the righteous fall seven times, they rise again, but the wicked stumble when calamity strikes."
Proverbs 24:16

BEYOND THE SCOREBOARD

When the **Ohio State Buckeyes** suffered a tough loss to archrival Michigan on November 30, 2024, and missed the College Football Playoff, the setback stunned the world. The loss hit hard. The team faced criticism, hurt pride, and intense public scrutiny. For a team used to national title conversations, the blow was more than physical—it tested their identity, unity, and belief in one another. But what happened next wasn't just a legendary comeback; it was a spiritual revival. In August 2024, over 800 students gathered on the Ohio State campus for a football team-led worship night, organized by players like Kamryn Babb, TreVeyon Henderson, and Emeka Egbuka. Players shared powerful testimonies of how Christ had carried them through injuries, mental battles, public pressure, and criticism. The Buckeyes didn't just want to win games—they wanted to glorify God with their lives.

When the 2024/2025 season kicked off, the Buckeyes looked different—not just in strength and strategy, but in character and faith. That faith fueled a redemption run that brought them back into title contention. The Buckeyes dominated through the Playoffs—defeating top-seeded Oregon and TCU—and culminated in a National Championship win over Notre Dame. This comeback exemplifies *"Though the righteous fall seven times, they rise again...".* Their fall in 2024 wasn't final—they believed, rebuilt, and submitted themselves to a higher purpose. Proverbs 24:16 isn't just about physical recovery. It's about trusting God enough to get up when you fall—again and again.

WEEKLY GAME PLAN

Reflection: *When things fall apart—your season, your confidence, your starting spot—how do you respond? Do you shrink and turn inward, or do you lean into your faith and rise up?*

_____

_____

_____

Challenge: Write down a "setback" you've experienced this season. Next to it, write a verse (like Micah 7:8) and one positive action goal to keep pressing forward.

THE PRAYER ZONE

Heavenly Father, thank You for picking me up every time I fall. Help me stay faithful and full of belief, even when I'm knocked down. Remind me that rising again isn't about being perfect—it's about trusting You in the process. **Amen.**

24

RISE WITH RESILIENCE

"Though I have fallen, I will rise. Though I sit in darkness, the Lord will be my light."
Micah 7:8

BEYOND THE SCOREBOARD

In the world of pro golf, mental strength is everything—and **Justin Thomas** knows it firsthand. After a meteoric rise in 2017, including a historic 59 and a major championship win, Justin hit an unexpected slump. Injuries, missed cuts, and intense pressure to perform pulled him into a dark season. Justin began wrestling with anxiety and depression—the once high-pressure golfer was now struggling mentally. He battled internal criticism, self-doubt, and emotional burnout. His swing suffered. But Justin didn't stay down. He was open about his faith, sharing Scripture, leaning on prayer, and recognizing that his identity came from God, not golf. Through Christian mentors, prayer, and devoting time in Scripture, Justin found the strength to keep swinging even when the results didn't show it. Slowly, he rebuilt himself. In 2022, Justin returned with an extraordinary win at the Masters, claiming the Green Jacket and overcoming not just competition, but his internal battles. Justin has stated: *"God didn't give me a spirit of fear... He gives me power, love, and self-discipline,"* reminding us that real strength comes from reliance on Him.

Micah 7:8 echoes Justin's journey: a reminder that setbacks don't mean God has left you. *"Though I have fallen, I will rise."* It's a promise of resilience because God is faithful. Resilience isn't avoiding the fall—it's choosing to get back up, fulfilled with faith. Even in darkness, when you feel unseen or off-track, the Lord becomes your light, guiding you through recovery and into victory. Remember, your setbacks don't define your entire story. Resilience is faith in action—bouncing back when others expect you to stay down. Your true strength is found when you lean on God's light, rise again, and step forward, growing in your spirit and your sport.

WEEKLY GAME PLAN

Reflection: *What does rising up with God's strength look like in your sport, and how might that change the way you respond to setbacks?*

_____

_____

_____

Challenge: Write down one area where you feel stuck or discouraged. Then beside it, write *"God's light leads me through."* Pray over that struggle every day this week—and keep showing up with faith and resilience.

THE PRAYER ZONE

Thank You, God, for never giving up on me—even when I fall. Help me rise with resilience and trust You as my light in the dark. **Amen.**

25

RECOVER, RELEASE, & REBUILD

"But he said to me, 'My grace is sufficient for you, for my power is made perfect in weakness.'"
2 Corinthians 12:9

BEYOND THE SCOREBOARD

In sports, bouncing back from a physical injury is tough—but healing from a mental and emotional setback can feel even harder. **Kevin Love**, NBA All-Star and 2016 Champion, reached the top of his game—yet behind the scenes, he was battling anxiety, panic attacks, and depression. One night during a game, it overwhelmed him. That was a turning point in this life—not just for his mental health, but for his faith. Instead of hiding, Kevin chose to recover openly. He released the fear of judgment and embraced the grace God freely gives. He later shared that he started seeing a Christian therapist, reading Scripture again, and leaning into his faith. *"You heal when you're honest—with yourself and with God,"* Kevin said. His willingness to be vulnerable helped countless others do the same.

Kevin's story shows that recovery isn't weakness—it's strength through surrender. It's letting go of what broke you and rebuilding with God's help. 2 Corinthians 12:9 reminds us that God's power shows up most when we feel the weakest. That's when His grace carries us. Athlete, setbacks are real. But they don't get the final word. With God, you can recover. You can release the weight of the shame, stress, or pain. Then you can rebuild—not just your performance, but your inner peace. What you release in faith, He can restore with power. Let His grace write your comeback.

WEEKLY GAME PLAN

Reflection: *Is there something—an injury, failure, or fear—you've been carrying that God is inviting you to release? How can you surrender that burden to God, release it, and allow Him to rebuild your heart and your mindset?*

Challenge: Take 10 minutes each day to talk to God about the struggles you've been trying to carry alone. Write them down here or in a journal and ask God to help you release them. Then pray that God allows you to start rebuilding—spiritually, mentally, and physically—with His strength.

THE PRAYER ZONE

Heavenly Father, thank You for Your grace that meets me in my weakness. When I feel weak, You make me strong. Help me release every disappointment to You and trust that You're working behind the scenes to renew and rebuild me. **Amen.**

26

HEART OF A CHAMPION

"But he knows the way that I take; when he has tested me, I will come forth as gold."
Job 23:10

BEYOND THE SCOREBOARD

Champions aren't just built by trophies—they're forged in fire. For quarterback **Alex Smith**, that fire came on November 18, 2018, when he suffered a catastrophic spiral fracture to his right leg during a Washington Redskins game. The injury shattered more than bone—it nearly cost him his life. Seventeen surgeries, a life-threatening infection, and 18 months in a metal fixator left doctors wondering if he'd ever walk again, let alone play football. But Alex didn't give up. He leaned into his faith and turned to God for hope and direction. Alex said, *"I know this is not the end of my story. God's not done with me yet."* Through excruciating rehab, mental struggles, and public doubt, Alex chose to believe God still had a purpose. Smith revealed that prayer, Scripture, and spiritual conversations were central to his healing. He believed in a bigger picture: that God could use his story to inspire others.

When Alex returned to the NFL field in 2020, it was more than a comeback—it was a testimony. A testimony that God can bring righteousness from brokenness, strength from suffering, and purpose from pain. Against all odds, Smith returned to the field mid-season and led Washington to a division title, earning the 2020 NFL Comeback Player of the Year.

As an athlete, you will face setbacks. But God can use that season to rebuild something more substantial in you. Like Alex, let your scars become your strength. Let your trials bring forth spiritual gold. Smith's story is truly one of a Heart of a Champion—one that beats strong because it trusts fully in the One who makes all things new.

WEEKLY GAME PLAN

Reflection: *What trials have tested your faith or confidence in your sport? How can you trust God to bring purpose out of your pain?*

_____

_____

_____

Challenge: Reflect on an area where you've faced a setback or disappointment. Write down three things you can do to rebuild stronger, mentally and spiritually. Pray before every practice or game, asking God for the strength to persevere.

THE PRAYER ZONE

Lord, thank You for being with me in hard seasons. When things feel broken, help me remember that You're still writing my story. Give me a heart of a champion— the strength to rebuild, courage to keep going, and faith to believe that You are forging something new in me. **Amen.**

CHAPTER 7:
COMMITMENT & MENTAL TOUGHNESS

27

ALL IN FOR CHRIST

"Commit to the Lord whatever you do, and he will establish your plans."
Proverbs 16:3

BEYOND THE SCOREBOARD

Maria Fassi isn't just known for her powerful swing—she's known for her powerful faith. The Mexican-born LPGA golfer burst onto the professional scene with poise, grit, and a deep sense of purpose. But behind her exceptional drive and distance is a quiet strength rooted in Christ. She's a model of unwavering commitment. Six days a week, even during the offseason, she hits the gym hard with explosive lunges, squats, and deadlift—the foundation of her massive drives off the tee. Twice-a-day sessions help build power and precision. She pairs intense training with mobility work—yoga and Pilates, to increase flexibility and sharpen her mental game.

While rising through the amateur and collegiate ranks, Maria constantly pointed her success back to God. *"I want my game to be a testimony,"* she said in an interview. *"Not just of hard work, but of who I play for."* Her Bible always travels with her, and prayer is part of her daily routine. When tournament stress hits, Maria leans on Scripture and prayer, centering her heart before every round. Even when scores dip or pressure hits, her heart stays steady—because she's already committed the outcome to the Lord.

Proverbs 16:3 challenges us: commit everything to the Lord, and He will guide your path. Being "All In for Christ" means more than hours in the gym or reps at practice. It means starting and ending each session with a heart surrendered—trusting God with both your game and your identity. When you commit everything to the Lord and pray through the grind, He will establish more than your plans. He will shape your character.

WEEKLY GAME PLAN

Reflection: *What part of your daily training or game do you find hard to fully commit to? How would surrendering that area to God bring you peace or purpose?*

_____

_____

_____

Challenge: This week, decide on one part of your routine—whether it's morning drills, stretch time, or a hydration habit—and approach it with intention as an offering to God. Stick with it daily.

THE PRAYER ZONE

Thank You, God, that every swing and every rep can be an act of worship. Help me commit my training, my time, and my effort entirely to You. **Amen.**

28

GRIT OVER QUIT

"I can do all things through Christ who strengthens me."
Philippians 4:13

BEYOND THE SCOREBOARD

Running a marathon isn't just about fast legs—it's about a fierce heart. Few athletes show that better than **Ryan Hall**, the fastest American marathoner in history, and a bold follower of Christ. Ryan became the first U.S. runner to break the one-hour barrier in the half-marathon and posted one of the top marathon times in Boston history. But what made him stand out wasn't just his speed—it was his spiritual grit.

Hall trained with unwavering intensity, logging over 100 miles a week, often battling exhaustion and injury. But through every setback, Ryan leaned hard on his faith, saying, *"God is my coach, my trainer, my everything."* His mental toughness didn't come from pushing past pain alone—it came from daily surrender, constant prayer, and trusting that God was using the struggles to refine him.

Philippians 4:13 is more than a slogan—it's a declaration of where your true strength lies. Mental toughness doesn't mean you never feel weak. It means you know where to run to when you do feel weak—straight to the One who empowers you to endure.

Young athlete, grit isn't about going solo—it's about relying on God when your legs want to quit, your lungs burn, and the finish line feels far away. Give it to God and lean into Him. You'll find a strength the world can't give you and a perseverance that won't back down.

WEEKLY GAME PLAN

Reflection: *When you face tough moments in training, competition, or life, do you rely on your own strength—or do you turn to God to power you through? What would it look like to trust Him with your exhaustion, your setbacks, or your pain?*

_____

_____

_____

Challenge: This week, choose one hard thing in your sport that you usually avoid—whether it's conditioning, mindset work, or a tough conversation with a coach. Commit to doing it with grit and grace. Before you start, say a short prayer asking God to strengthen you through it.

THE PRAYER ZONE

Heavenly Father, thank You for giving me strength that lasts beyond my limits. When I feel tired or discouraged, help me lean on You to power through, instead of giving up. Teach me to press on with grit, faith, and purpose. **Amen.**

29

UNBREAKABLE SPIRIT

"We are hard pressed on every side, but not crushed; perplexed, but not in despair; persecuted, but not abandoned; struck down, but not destroyed."
2 Corinthians 4:8–9

BEYOND THE SCOREBOARD

Born without fibulas, ankles, and heels, **Jessica Long**—one of the most decorated Paralympians of all time—was adopted from a Siberian orphanage and underwent over 25 surgeries before she turned 18. Yet she didn't let adversity write her story. She rewrote it with faith, fight, and fire.

With over 20 medals, Jessica is well known for her dominance in the pool. But what truly defines Jessica is the strength of her unshakable spirit in Christ. *"My identity is not found in winning medals,"* she's said. *"It's found in who I am in Jesus."*

Jessica has openly shared how she battled overcoming physical limitations, self-doubt, body image issues, and bullying growing up. Through it all, she clung to Scripture and prayer. Her incredible journey is all about showing the power of a surrendered heart, trusting God when life feels unfair, and standing firm in His purpose.

As a young athlete, it's important to know that being unbreakable doesn't mean being perfect. It means trusting God to hold you together when life tries to break you apart. Let Him be your anchor. With Him, your strength will never fail, and your spirit will not be broken.

WEEKLY GAME PLAN

Reflection: *What's an area in your life or sport where you feel discouraged or all the odds are stacked against you? How can you remind yourself that your strength doesn't come from your body or circumstances—but from God's Spirit inside you?*

_____

_____

_____

Challenge: This week, write down one tough situation you're facing and choose a Bible verse to pray over it daily. When setbacks come—whether it's a tough call, a rough practice, or a personal struggle—say aloud: *"I may be pressed, but I am not crushed. God's not done with me. He has given me an unbreakable spirit."*

THE PRAYER ZONE

Thank You, God, for never leaving me—even when I feel knocked down or broken. Give me an unbreakable spirit like Jessica Long and a heart that trusts You through every trial. Help me rise stronger through faith and remind me that I'm never defeated when I walk with You. **Amen.**

30

LOCKED IN & LOYAL

"Do you not know that in a race all the runners run, but only one gets the prize? Run in such a way as to get the prize. Everyone who competes in the games goes into strict training."
1 Corinthians 9:24–25

BEYOND THE SCOREBOARD

Locked in. That's what they called **Michael Phelps**—laser-focused, relentlessly driven, and unwilling to let distractions derail his goals. From a young age, Phelps set his sights high on Olympic greatness and trained with an intensity and commitment most athletes couldn't match. Phelps showed unmatched commitment by training six hours a day, 365 days a year, for over five years without missing a single practice. His strict nutritional intake of of 10,000–12,000 calories a day was tailored to support his heavy workload. He pushed through grueling physical exhaustion and mental strain to stay laser-focused on his Olympic goals. Even during times of personal struggle and pressure, he displayed mental toughness by continuing to show up, stay disciplined, and chased excellence with relentless determination. What the world didn't always see was the internal war he fought: mental health battles, anxiety, pressure, and temptations to quit. Instead of giving up, Phelps made a decision—to stay loyal to his calling, lean on the Lord, and push through the struggles, day after day, lap after lap. Phelps began speaking openly about his faith and healing. After hitting rock bottom in 2014, he found support through faith-based rehab and spiritual mentoring. He credits his turnaround to trusting God's grace, saying, *"The only reason I'm alive today is because I found God."*

1 Corinthians 9:24 reminds us: if you're going to run the race, run to win—with eternal purpose. For young athletes, this means staying committed and locked into the discipline God has called you to and being loyal to the journey He's laid out before you.

WEEKLY GAME PLAN

Reflection: *What does it look like for you to stay locked in on your goals and remain loyal to the discipline even when it's hard or inconvenient?*

_____

_____

_____

Challenge: This week, choose one discipline in your training and stick to it. When you feel like quitting, remind yourself: champions are built in the moments no one sees. Stay committed even when it's hard.

THE PRAYER ZONE

Thank You, God, for giving me the opportunities to grow through sports. Help me stay focused and push forward with mental toughness, even when it's tough. Teach me to be loyal to Your plans and fully committed to everything I do. **Amen.**

SECTION III: TEAM VALUES & IMPACT

(WEEKS 31 - 42)

The most memorable teams aren't just made up of stars—they're built on a brotherhood of trust, humility, unity, and a shared purpose. This section of devotions teaches young athletes how to lead with influence, serve with humility, lift others, and value the success of the team over personal glory. Through lessons on sacrifice, selflessness, and forgiveness, you will learn how to create a lasting impact both on and off the field by reflecting Christ in every interaction.

CHAPTER 8: TEAMWORK & UNITY

31

ONE BODY, ONE GOAL

"Then make my joy complete by being like-minded, having the same love, being one in spirit and of one mind."
Philippians 2:2

BEYOND THE SCOREBOARD

Their stat sheets were impressive, but it was the brotherhood anchored in Christ that made the **2018 Clemson Tigers** truly unstoppable. Under Coach Dabo Swinney, the team built a culture rooted in faith, family, and unbreakable unity. Swinney openly professed his faith in Jesus Christ and created a locker room camaraderie where prayer, brotherhood, and accountability were as fundamental to their success as their game plans. Team unity wasn't forced—it was formed through mutual trust, purpose, and a shared belief in Christ. From team chapels to baptisms, the Tigers bonded deeper than just through football. Clemson's legendary "Power Rangers" defensive line—Christian Wilkins, Clelin Ferrell, Austin Bryant, and Dexter Lawrence—all could have entered the NFL early in 2017. Unselfishly, they chose to return, not for personal glory, but to chase a national title together. This unwavering unity showed in their unselfish play and mutual support—starters cheering backups, defense celebrating offense, and a team playing for something greater than themselves. With a 15–0 Record in 2018, Clemson became the first modern college football team to go 15–0 since 1897. They finished the season as the ACC Champions and with a National Championship Victory.

Philippians 2:2 reminds us that Christ-centered unity means aligning our hearts and minds. When athletes pursue the same mission—loving one another and glorifying God—the unstoppable happens. Whether you're on the bench or in the spotlight, unity means showing up for your teammates, celebrating their success, and keeping your eyes on the greater purpose: reflecting Jesus.

WEEKLY GAME PLAN

Reflection: *Think about how your words, actions, and attitude either build unity or break it. Explain.*

_____

_____

_____

Challenge: Go out of your way to encourage a teammate who's struggling by celebrating them instead of focusing on your own role. Be the kind of teammate who lifts others higher.

THE PRAYER ZONE

Father, thank You for the team You've placed me on. Please help me be a unifier, not a divider. Whether I'm starting or sitting, let me serve my teammates with a grateful heart and glorify You in every play. **Amen.**

32

MORE THAN THE GAME

"Do nothing out of selfish ambition or vain conceit. Rather, in humility value others above yourselves, not looking to your own interests but each of you to the interests of the others."
Philippians 2:3—4

BEYOND THE SCOREBOARD

In championship sports, glory often goes to the biggest scorer or the flashiest play. But the **U.S. Women's National Soccer Team(USWNT),** especially during their dominant 2015 and 2019 World Cup runs, proved that true greatness comes from playing for something bigger than yourself. Led by Christ-centered athletes like Tobin Heath, Julie Ertz, and Christen Press, the team embodied humility, unity, and purpose. Ertz was known not just for goals and lifting teammates up, but for doing the dirty work—defending, pressing, assisting—without craving attention or headlines. Tobin Heath, known for her creative footwork, was also vocal about her faith, saying, *"Soccer is not who I am, it's what I do. I'm a daughter of God, and I live to serve Him."* She openly shares her desire to use her sport to glorify Christ, not herself. The team had a collective mission and a culture of sacrifice: many times, the star players sat out so others could shine, and several took on support roles during injury recovery or lineup changes.

While the world watched their wins in awe, few saw the behind-the-scenes selflessness—players praying together, cheering from the bench, and making personal sacrifices to elevate the team. Their mission wasn't just to win, but to represent their country and their Creator with honor.

Philippians 2:3–4 reminds us that when we value the team over ourselves, God does big things through our obedience. Athletes who serve the mission, not themselves, don't just build teams—they build legacies.

WEEKLY GAME PLAN

Reflection: *Do I approach my team and sport with a servant's heart, or am I focused on my own spotlight? Am I willing to do the unseen or unglamorous work that helps my team succeed?*

Challenge: This week, intentionally celebrate someone else's success or volunteer for a support role that helps your team thrive.

THE PRAYER ZONE

Dear Lord, thank You for the gift of my team and the opportunity to play. Teach me to serve with humility, to lift others, and to reflect Your heart in how I train, compete, and support my teammates. Help me play for the mission, not for myself. **Amen.**

33

HUDDLE UP IN CHRIST

"And let us consider how we may spur one another on toward love and good deeds, not giving up meeting together... but encouraging one another."
Hebrews 10:24–25

BEYOND THE SCOREBOARD

Before they lifted the Lombardi Trophy, the **2017 Philadelphia Eagles** were already winning—in the locker room, in prayer circles, and in their bold pursuit of Christ as a unified team. That Super Bowl–winning team was stacked with gifted players, but what truly set them apart was their spiritual brotherhood. Led by bold believers like Carson Wentz, Nick Foles, Zach Ertz, Trey Burton, and Chris Maragos, the team held weekly Bible studies, baptized teammates in the recovery pool, and constantly encouraged each other in their faith. When Carson Wentz suffered a season-ending injury, Nick Foles stepped in and led the team all the way to a Super Bowl victory but never took the credit. Instead, he said, *"I want to glorify God in everything I do. Win or lose, I give Him the glory."* That mindset wasn't just his—it was a team culture rooted in Christ.

This verse reflects exactly what the Eagles modeled: a spiritual huddle where teammates encouraged, prayed, and spurred each other on—not just for a trophy, but for eternal impact. It's a call to every athlete: build more than a team—create a brotherhood in Christ.

When teammates stand together in prayer, encourage one another in challenging moments, and compete with a higher purpose, they form a spiritually unshakable team. Young athlete, this applies to you. Surround yourself with teammates and friends who lift you up in faith. Build huddles that aren't just about game plans, but about godly purpose. That's how championship cultures are built—from the inside out.

WEEKLY GAME PLAN

Reflection: *Do I have a spiritual huddle—a few teammates I can pray and grow with? How can I specifically bring faith into my team's culture this season?*

_____

_____

_____

Challenge: Start a simple team prayer before or after games and practices this week. Invite even one or two teammates to join you in prayer.

THE PRAYER ZONE

Thank You, God, for teammates who point me to You. Help me build a team culture that honors You through unity, love, and a bold faith. Make our huddle a place of worship and a brotherhood in Christ where You are always welcome. **Amen.**

34

WE OVER ME, ALWAYS

"Do nothing out of selfish ambition or vain conceit. Rather, in humility value others above yourselves, not looking to your own interests but each of you to the interests of the others."
Philippians 2:3–4

BEYOND THE SCOREBOARD

In a sport where personal stats often steal the spotlight, **Adam Wainwright** of the St. Louis Cardinals built his legacy on something more profound—humility, selflessness, and putting his team first. A devout Christian, Wainwright never chased individual glory. He stayed loyal to one franchise his entire career and consistently deflected praise to his teammates. Even as a star pitcher, he chose to mentor younger players and stepped aside when it benefited the team's future. In one powerful moment, Wainwright allowed a rookie to take his spot in a game he could've excelled, but rather, he said, *"This isn't about me. It's about what helps us win."* That's a powerful example of we over me. Wainwright also founded Big League Impact, which partners with other MLB players to fund food programs, medical aid, and clean water projects around the world. He uses his platform not to promote himself, but to rally others for a greater mission, modeling Philippians 2:3-4 in real life.

Philippians 2:3–4 teaches us to crush pride and choose humility. It challenges us to care more about team success than personal achievement. For young athletes, this means encouraging your teammates when they shine, passing instead of scoring when it's best for the team, and playing your role with excellence—whether you're the starter or cheering from the sideline. Winning teams are built on players who serve others. Champions in Christ are known not just for how they compete, but for how they lift others up. That's how you turn a game into a witness.

WEEKLY GAME PLAN

Reflection: *When was the last time you celebrated a teammate's win like it was your own? Are you willing to step back so someone else can step up for the benefit of the team?*

_____

_____

_____

Challenge: This week, look for one opportunity to put a teammate first above your own interests. That might mean passing instead of scoring, staying late to help someone train, or encouraging a teammate after a tough day. Make "we over me" your mindset.

THE PRAYER ZONE

My Lord, thank You for the teammates You've placed around me. Help me to serve with humility, play with selflessness, and lead with character. Teach me to value others above myself, just like Jesus did. **Amen.**

CHAPTER 9: LEADERSHIP & INFLUENCE

35

SHINE TO LEAD

"Let your light shine before others, that they may see your good deeds and glorify your Father in heaven."

Matthew 5:16

BEYOND THE SCOREBOARD

True leadership isn't about the spotlight—it's about light. Olympic snowboarder **Kelly Clark**, a five-time U.S. Olympian and gold medalist, led not just with her skill but with her undimmable light in Christ. Known as one of the greatest snowboarders in history, Clark also became known for her kindness, humility, and her quiet influence on younger athletes.

Her turning point came after overhearing another competitor say, *"God still loves you even if you don't win."* That moment sparked a journey of faith in Kelly that changed her life—and her leadership. From that point on, Clark began shining differently: helping others succeed, mentoring rookies, and carrying peace with her wherever she competed.

Matthew 5:16 teaches us to let our light shine, not for applause, but so others are drawn to the goodness of God. That's exactly what Kelly did.

She used her snowboarding platform to inspire others toward Christ—not just with talent, but with truth.

Young athlete, your light isn't your stat sheet—it's your attitude, your faith, and your example. Whether you're a team captain or the last one off the bench, when you choose integrity over ego and encouragement over envy, you shine. And when you shine, you lead.

WEEKLY GAME PLAN

Reflection: *What kind of example are you setting for your teammates? How can your light and faith be something others want to follow?*

_____

_____

_____

Challenge: This week, lead with your light. Find one way to serve or encourage without seeking recognition—and give God all the glory.

THE PRAYER ZONE

Thank You, God, for the light You've placed in me. Help me to shine with humility, kindness, and courage so others can see Your love through my actions. Make me a leader who reflects You. **Amen.**

36

CAPTAIN THE MISSION

"Be shepherds of God's flock that is under your care, watching over them—not because you must, but because you are willing... not lording it over those entrusted to you, but being examples to the flock."
1 Peter 5:2–3

BEYOND THE SCOREBOARD

Great captains don't just call the plays—they carry the mission. Olympic bobsledder **Elana Meyers Taylor** is a five-time medalist and one of the most decorated women in her sport. Her greatest impact may not be found on the podium, but rather, in how she leads her team with character, courage, and conviction.

As team captain for the U.S. bobsled team, Elana consistently led by example. She pushed the sled harder, trained longer, and showed up early to support rookies. More than that, she made it her mission to fight for equality, inclusion, and respect in her sport—even when it cost her comfort or popularity. As a bold Christian athlete, she often credits her strength and leadership to her faith in Christ, saying she strives to *"honor God in everything I do."*

1 Peter 5:2–3 reminds us that real leadership means shepherding others—not for power, but out of love. Elana didn't lead because she had to. She led because she knew God placed people in her care—and she answered that call with grit and grace.

As a young athlete, captaining the mission means showing up when others slack off, staying true when others give up, and leading from the front with humility and heart. Lead the mission for the greater good of the team, to lift others up, and shepherd your teammates to the Lord.

WEEKLY GAME PLAN

Reflection: *What kind of example are you setting for teammates who look up to you? Are you leading from the front or watching from the back?*

_____

_____

_____

Challenge: Find one way to lead quietly this week: help a teammate behind the scenes, offer encouragement, or pray for someone on your team who needs a little extra help.

THE PRAYER ZONE

Thank You, Heavenly Father, for trusting me to influence others. Help me to lead with humility, serve with joy, and stay committed to the mission You've given me. Use my leadership to Captain the Mission and point others to You. **Amen.**

37

SERVE FIRST, LEAD STRONG

"For even the Son of Man came not to be served but to serve, and to give his life as a ransom for many."
Mark 10:45

BEYOND THE SCOREBOARD

When the spotlight hits, many athletes chase stats, glory, and endorsement deals. However, **Jonathan Isaac**—forward for the Orlando Magic—has chosen a different playbook. His career is marked by exceptional talent and a willingness to sacrifice personal acclaim for a much greater purpose: honoring Christ and uplifting his team. Despite being a top NBA draft pick, Isaac has consistently downplayed individual achievements. He's known for prioritizing team defense over scoring and doing the gritty work that doesn't show up on social media highlight reels. Off the court, Isaac leads Bible studies with teammates and openly declares his faith, not for attention, but to serve others spiritually.

In 2020, while the league kneeled in protest, Isaac stood —not to oppose others, but to stand for Jesus. He did it quietly, respectfully, and boldly, sharing afterward that his hope for change comes through the Gospel alone. That moment wasn't for applause. It was a sacrificial act of service —to point others to Christ. He also launched UNITUS, a faith-forward sports brand created to equip Christian athletes to stand for truth.

Mark 10:45 reminds us that even Jesus didn't come to be served, but to serve. For young athletes, this means celebrating teammates' wins, sharing the ball, and remembering that every practice and game is an opportunity to serve, not shine. Like Isaac, you're most powerful when your play lifts others up. Great teams are built when egos take the bench—and Christ leads the charge.

WEEKLY GAME PLAN

Reflection: *Who around you needs encouragement or support today? In what ways can you serve your teammates more intentionally this week?*

_____

_____

_____

Challenge: Take one bold action this week that lifts someone else up —whether it's helping a teammate or standing up for what's right, even if you're standing alone.

THE PRAYER ZONE

God, thank You for the example of Jesus, who led by serving others. Help me lead like Him, with humility, courage, and integrity. Use my actions to serve my team and point my teammates to You. In Jesus' name, **Amen.**

38

LEAD LIKE JESUS

"Follow my example, as I follow the example of Christ."
1 Corinthians 11:1

BEYOND THE SCOREBOARD

David Wise isn't just the King of Winter Olympic gold medals—he's a champion of character. The first Olympic champion in men's freestyle halfpipe (2014, 2018) and a multi-time X-Games winner, David credits his faith for fueling his mountaintop success. He said, *"Skiing for me has always been my act of worship to God... I don't treat my sport as something that brings glory to me, but to the Creator."* While many individual athletes get caught up in chasing personal fame, David didn't let his success and limelight go to his head. Instead, he used it to lead others with humility and heart. Consistently, he mentored young skiers through Bible study, encouraged others through life's pressures, and modeled Christlike strength through personal trials—injuries, family loss, sponsor cutbacks—never using the setbacks for sympathy, but for growing more faithful to God. He once shared that after shifting from performing for glory to living for God, *"I almost couldn't be beaten"*—not from arrogance, but from inner peace and purpose. Wise isn't flashy about it. He's faithful. He often says his identity isn't found in gold medals but in being a child of God. That kind of humble strength is rare—and powerful.

In 1 Corinthians 11:1, St. Paul boldly tells believers to follow his example as he follows Christ. That's precisely what David Wise does. He invites others to observe his faith in action, then points them to the One he follows. Leadership through example. For young athletes, this is a game-changer. Leadership isn't reserved for captains or all-stars. You can also lead today—by how you train, encourage, forgive, and compete. When you live like Jesus, you lead like Him too.

WEEKLY GAME PLAN

Reflection: *Are you leading by example, or just expecting others to follow? What is one way you can reflect Jesus in how you lead teammates this week?*

_____

_____

_____

Challenge: Commit to one intentional act of Christ-like leadership—pray before practice, uplift a discouraged teammate, or own a mistake with humility.

THE PRAYER ZONE

Thank You, Lord, for showing us the ultimate example of servant leadership. Help me lead like Jesus—not through power, but through love, integrity, and example. Let others see You in the way I train, speak, and serve. **Amen.**

CHAPTER 10: SACRIFICE & SELFLESSNESS

39

MISSION OVER ME

"For to me to live is Christ, and to die is gain."
Philippians 1:21

BEYOND THE SCOREBOARD

When most athletes chase stats and spotlight, **Kenzie Koerber** chases something bigger—God's mission. As a volleyball player at BYU, Kenzie was one of the top volleyball players in the nation—an All-American and Pac-12 Player of the Year. But her greatest decision wasn't about titles or trophies. After a successful career at the University of Utah, Kenzie chose to transfer to BYU—not for more fame, but to grow her faith and surround herself with teammates who shared her purpose. She gave up the spotlight to follow God's direction.

That's what Paul meant in Philippians 1:21: to live is to follow Christ. Kenzie didn't just say it—she lived it. At BYU, she used her platform to mentor younger athletes and encourage her team. She made it clear: her identity wasn't found in volleyball, but in Jesus. Every serve, every huddle, every post-game moment pointed to something greater than herself.

Philippians 1:21 reminds us that life—yes, even sports—isn't about self-glory. It's about reflecting Christ and pointing others to Him. When you put God's mission over personal ambition, you lead in a way that changes teams and touches hearts. That's a kind of influence that outlasts trophies.

Being mission-minded doesn't mean playing small—it means playing with purpose. Like Kenzie, you can hustle hard and lead well, not to make a name for yourself, but to make Jesus known.

WEEKLY GAME PLAN

Reflection: *What's one area in your sport where you've made it about you instead of God? How can you use your role—starter or bench, captain or rookie—to serve a greater purpose?*

_____

_____

_____

Challenge: This week, choose to support a teammate without expecting credit. Whether it's helping them improve a shot or simply encouraging them, let your actions say: *"I'm here for more than just me."*

THE PRAYER ZONE

Thank You, God, for giving me a mission bigger than winning. Help me put You first, my teammates second, and myself last. May my attitude reflect Your love, and my actions point to You. **Amen.**

40

SACRIFICE FOR THE GREATER GOOD

"Greater love has no one than this: to lay down one's life for one's friends."
John 15:13

BEYOND THE SCOREBOARD

Driven by something greater than gold, **Allyson Felix** used her speed to serve others. At the height of her career, she sacrificed sponsorships, comfort, and even her body to stand up for something bigger than herself. In 2018, when Felix became a mother, she publicly challenged Nike's policy of reducing female athletes' pay during maternity. Felix soon realized that elite female athletes often faced financial penalties or lost contracts when starting families. Her stand cost her financially, but she chose the greater good, to use her platform to protect and empower future generations of female athletes. Her bold stand against Nike sparked change—not just for her sake, but for countless women in sports.

John 15:13 reminds us sacrifice isn't always about giving up your life for something. Sacrifice is about giving up status, security, or spotlight for the sake of others. Allyson gave up millions of dollars in endorsements to shine a light on injustice and protect future athletes. After Nike dropped her endorsement, Felix later partnered with Athleta to create her own brand of shoes. She helped launch initiatives to support women's health and equity in sports. Her sacrifice wasn't about her—it was about change for the greater good.

Young athlete, being a champion isn't just about medals—it's about the impact you leave on others. Sacrifice for the greater good might mean passing on the spotlight, helping a struggling teammate instead of crafting your own skills, or speaking up when it's risky.

WEEKLY GAME PLAN

Reflection: *Am I playing for just myself, or for something greater than me? Explain.*

_____

_____

_____

Challenge: This week, find one opportunity to serve or support a teammate—even if it means stepping back from the spotlight. That could be giving up a starting spot, helping a teammate train, or simply encouraging someone who's struggling.

THE PRAYER ZONE

Heavenly Father, thank You for showing us the ultimate example of sacrifice through Jesus. Please help me play with a heart that puts others before myself. Teach me to lead with humility, serve with joy, and give up what's comfortable if it means helping someone else grow. **Amen.**

41

SURRENDER THE SPOTLIGHT

"He must become greater; I must become less."
John 3:30

BEYOND THE SCOREBOARD

In a league filled with highlight reels, social media posts, and self-promotion, former NFL tight end **Benjamin Watson** lived with a different goal: glorifying God, not himself. Throughout his 15-year career with the Patriots, Saints, and Ravens, Watson made headlines for more than his touchdowns and stats—he made his faith publicly known by consistently pointing the spotlight to Christ.

Despite being a Super Bowl champion, Watson never sought fame for its own sake. After scoring touchdowns, he often knelt in prayer. After press conferences, he redirected attention to his faith and family. Even in retirement, he's used his influence to serve, speak out for justice, and lead with humility. In his words: *"My job isn't just to play football. It's to be a witness for Christ."*

John 3:30 perfectly reflects this mindset: *"He must become greater; I must become less."* John the Baptist knew his role wasn't to be the star prophet—it was to prepare the way for Jesus. Watson has consistently modeled that same humility in the spotlight of professional sports. As a young athlete, you may be praised for your stats, talent, perfect form, or hustle. But don't let the spotlight blind you. Use it to shine God's light. Real greatness is found in surrender, selflessness, and sacrifice—when you lay down pride, God lifts up your purpose. Let your talents and influence point others to Jesus.

WEEKLY GAME PLAN

Reflection: *Where in your sport do you feel pressure to make it all about you? In what way can you redirect the spotlight back to God this week?*

_____

_____

_____

Challenge: Choose one way to step away from the spotlight and let another player shine. When you receive compliments or praise this week, redirect the spotlight to point back to God.

THE PRAYER ZONE

Father, thank You for the gifts You've given me. Help me remember that my talents are from You and for You. Teach me to play with boldness but walk with humility, always pointing the spotlight to You and Your glory. **Amen.**

42

SUCCESS THROUGH SACRIFICE

"Offer your bodies as a living sacrifice, holy and pleasing to God—this is your true and proper worship."
Romans 12:1

BEYOND THE SCOREBOARD

Stephen Curry is an exceptional Christian individual who deserves to be recognized more than once in this devotional—not only for his Kingdom Minded Athlete mentality (Devotion #4), but also for being a perfect example of Success Through Sacrifice. Curry may be known for revolutionizing the game of basketball with his deep shooting range and MVP performances. Still, his success was built on pure sacrifice, not shortcuts. Early in his journey, Curry was overlooked by major college programs and doubted because of his size. Instead of giving in to the noise and negativity, he dedicated himself to relentless training—waking up early, perfecting his form, pushing through fatigue, and refining every detail of his craft. Behind the scenes, he sacrificed time, comfort, and popularity to become a master of his game.

But what was his greatest sacrifice? Submitting his success to God. Curry famously writes *"I can do all things"* on his shoes—not as a boast, but as a reminder that his strength and success come from Christ. He tithes (gives a portion of his weekly income to God), leads with humility, and has said, *"The Lord has blessed me with talents to play this game, but I still have to work and sacrifice to honor Him."*

Romans 12:1 reminds us that our lives—our practices, games, studies, choices, and effort—are all sacrificial offerings to God. When you give your time, sweat, tears, and best effort, not just for stats but as worship, that's sacrifice with purpose. Success through daily sacrifice isn't easy. But like Steph, if you give everything for God's glory, He'll use your game to make an eternal impact on you and those around you.

WEEKLY GAME PLAN

Reflection: *What comfort, habit, or distraction might God be asking you to sacrifice this week to reach your potential and honor Him more?*

_____

_____

_____

Challenge: This week, choose one thing to give up for the sake of your sport and spiritual growth—whether it's screen time, junk food, or laziness in workouts. Offer it up as a sacrifice to the Lord.

THE PRAYER ZONE

Dear God, thank You for allowing me to grow through sacrifice. Help me train and play with the mindset of worshiping You. I offer everything to you, Lord— my effort, my discipline, my heart, and my success. **Amen.**

SECTION IV: LIVING LIKE CHRIST

(WEEKS 43 - 52)

Your legacy as an athlete isn't just about stats alone. It's about how you reflect Christ in everything you do. This set of devotions challenges rising athletes to live boldly, forgive quickly, and lead with humility, even when no one is watching. You will discover, through powerful examples of grace, forgiveness, and unshakable faith, how to be a light for Christ in your sport—becoming a faithful witness through the way you speak, act, and carry yourself far beyond your sport.

CHAPTER 11: GRACE & FORGIVENESS

43

GRACE IN DEFEAT

"But he said to me, 'My grace is sufficient for you, for my power is made perfect in weakness.'"
2 Corinthians 12:9

BEYOND THE SCOREBOARD

In July 2019, at the World Aquatics Championships in Gwangju, **Katie Ledecky,** the most decorated female Olympic swimmer in history, faced a rare setback. In the women's 400m freestyle final, Ariarne Titmus (Australian gold medalist) overtook her in the last 50 meters, leaving Katie with a silver medal. The cameras zoomed in, expecting frustration, blame, and disappointment. But Katie responded with quiet grace. She smiled, hugged her competitor, and gave glory to God. She later said, *"I'm thankful for the opportunity. God's plan is always good."* That's grace in defeat! Katie knew her worth wasn't defined by one loss. Her strength came from something deeper than gold medals—it came from Christ.

2 Corinthians 12:9 reminds us that God's power shines brightest in our weakest moments. When things don't go as planned—when our best isn't good enough—God's grace fills the gap. Katie's reaction—no excuses, no

anger, just reset—showed humility and grace under pressure. She trusted God's grace and believed there was purpose in every step back. That's the power of grace in defeat: it reveals our dependence on God and allows us to grow in character.

Losing hurts. But how you handle it reveals your true character. Can you show sportsmanship after a big loss? Can you smile and stay positive? Can you worship and give glory to God even in disappointment? That's where grace becomes real.

WEEKLY GAME PLAN

Reflection: *Do I see failure as a lesson—or just defeat? Do I get bitter or better when I fail? How can I do better in showing God's grace in my mistakes?*

_____

_____

_____

Challenge: After your next tough game or loss, don't let it break you. Congratulate the winner. Encourage a teammate. Thank a coach. Say a prayer of gratitude and let others see God's grace in how you respond to defeat.

THE PRAYER ZONE

Heavenly Father, thank You for your gift of grace in tough times. Please give me grace when things don't go my way. Help me lose with courage, humility, and trust. Remind me that my worth is in You and not defined by the scoreboard or a loss. **Amen.**

44

RISE WHEN YOU FALL

"The Lord upholds all who fall and lifts up all who are bowed down."
Psalm 145:14

BEYOND THE SCOREBOARD

When **David Boudia** stood on the Olympic platform, millions saw a polished champion. However, few knew the fall it took to get there. Early in his diving career, Boudia's identity was wrapped in medals, rankings, and pressure. But soon the weight of performance began to crush him with anxiety and emptiness. After a disappointing showing at the 2008 Olympics, David hit a spiritual rock bottom—then he encountered God's grace.

Boudia gave his life to Christ in 2010, discovering that his worth wasn't in his dives, but rather, in being a child of God. That shift in mindset changed his faith, and it changed how he competed. In 2012, he stunned the world by winning gold in the 10-meter platform. But more powerful than his comeback performance was the peace he carried. He no longer dove for approval—he dove from a place of freedom.

Psalm 145:14 reminds us that when we fall, God doesn't leave us in the pit. He lifts us, not just physically, but spiritually restoring our hope, purpose, and confidence. Falling doesn't make you a failure; staying down does. With Christ, even failure becomes part of your growth story.

As a young athlete, when you stumble in sports—or in life—it's important to lean into God's grace. He's not tallying your mistakes. He's offering a hand to help you rise up, stronger and more resilient than before.

WEEKLY GAME PLAN

Reflection: *Think back on a failure or setback you have experienced recently, and how did you respond—by staying down or rising up with God's help?*

_____

_____

_____

Challenge: When you fall short—miss a shot, lose a game, or mess up—pause and pray. Then rise up with grace and humility, not excuses.

THE PRAYER ZONE

Thank You, Lord, for never giving up on me. When I fall, remind me that Your grace is bigger than my failure. Help me rise up and reflect Your character. **Amen.**

45

LET GO, MOVE FORWARD

"Forget the former things; do not dwell on the past. See, I am doing a new thing! Now it springs up; do you not perceive it?"
Isaiah 43:18–19

BEYOND THE SCOREBOARD

In the high-stakes world of Olympic softball, the pressure to be perfect can weigh heavily on a player's mind. For Team USA's **Ali Aguilar**, it was more than just about winning—it was about identity. Early in her career, Ali battled the pressure of performance, believing her worth was tied to flawless play. But in the background, God was writing a different story—one of grace, not perfection. Ali has spoken about the inner war between expectation and freedom. After games where she struck out or made an error, shame and self-doubt would creep in. However, instead of staying stuck in the past, Ali learned to release her failures to God, trusting that His love doesn't depend on batting averages or perfect plays. Her breakthrough came when she surrendered the scoreboard and leaned fully into her faith, realizing she truly plays for an Audience of One.

The Scripture reminds us to let go of what's behind us—mistakes, guilt, regret, doubt—and trust the "new thing" God is doing to rebuild us behind the scenes. This doesn't mean ignoring our failures and imperfections but surrendering them to God, so they don't define us and hold us back. God's grace creates room for forgiveness and growth, not shame.

Young athletes must learn to forgive themselves, shake off past errors, and move forward. That's what real strength looks like—not never falling, but getting back up, rising above the mistakes, letting them go, moving forward with grace, and playing freely for the love of the game.

WEEKLY GAME PLAN

Reflection: *When you make a mistake in your sport, do you tend to replay it in your head or release it to God? What's one area of your game where God might be inviting you to stop dwelling on the past and trust His grace for a fresh start?*

_____

_____

_____

Challenge: This week, when you mess up, pause and pray Isaiah 43:18–19. Say out loud, *"God is doing a new thing in me."* Then let it go and quickly move forward with confidence.

THE PRAYER ZONE

God, Thank You for Your grace that gives me afresh start every day. Help me to let go of my past failures and trust that You are always doing new work in my life. **Amen.**

46

COMPOSED IN CHRIST

"But seek first his kingdom and his righteousness, and all these things will be given to you as well."
Proverbs 19:11

BEYOND THE SCOREBOARD

Trevor Rosenthal, an MLB pitcher and devoted Christian, is no stranger to pressure. From closing out high-stakes playoff games to enduring multiple injuries and surgeries, Rosenthal has lived through the highs and lows of professional sports. After a stellar 2015 season with the St. Louis Cardinals, his career took a dramatic detour. He faced a string of challenges—Tommy John surgery, inconsistent performances on the mound, and multiple team changes that could've shaken his confidence. Yet through it all, he turned to his faith and trusted that God was still writing his story. What made Trevor's comeback so powerful wasn't just his performance. It was the calm strength he showed, the humility in how he handled setbacks, and the unwavering trust he placed in God along the way. Trevor never lashed out, blamed others, or gave up. Instead, he consistently gave credit to God, relied on his faith community, and modeled grace in how he handled public criticism and personal frustration. His Instagram posts and interviews often referenced how prayer and Scripture kept him grounded when things didn't go his way. He said, *"The game doesn't define me. Christ does."*

Proverbs 19:11 teaches us that wisdom leads to patience and that true strength lies in gracious restraint. For a young athlete, this means keeping your cool when you're benched, showing grace when calls don't go your way, or shaking hands with sportsmanship after a tough loss. Being composed in Christ means your character stays steady in good times and bad, because your heart is anchored in something greater than the scoreboard.

WEEKLY GAME PLAN

Reflection: *When times are bad, do you respond with patience and grace instead of frustration or anger? Explain.*

_____

_____

_____

Challenge: This week, when something doesn't go your way, pause, compose yourself, and choose patience. Pray in the moment instead of reacting. Practice being composed in Christ, not because you're ignoring the frustration, but because you're trusting God to shape you through it.

THE PRAYER ZONE

Heavenly Father, thank You for being my anchor in every storm. Help me stay calm and confident, even when the game doesn't go my way. Please give me the strength to respond with grace and the wisdom to be patient with my abilities. Teach me to be composed in Christ. **Amen.**

47

PLAY WITH A FORGIVING HEART

"Be kind and compassionate to one another, forgiving each other, just as in Christ God forgave you."
Ephesians 4:32

BEYOND THE SCOREBOARD

Caitlin Clark's rookie WNBA season has been a powerful real-life example of what it means to play with a forgiving heart. Despite being the most talked-about rookie in years, Caitlin Clark entered the WNBA under intense pressure. Most of the pressure came from the physical play, cold receptions, and even moments where fellow players seemed to target her for her fame. She faced aggressive defense, hard fouls, and what many called bullying behavior. Yet through it all, Caitlin kept her composure. She didn't lash out. She didn't retaliate. Instead, she said in interviews that she's *"focused on learning, staying composed, and letting her game speak."*

This attitude is the embodiment of Ephesians 4:32. Forgiveness isn't just saying "I forgive you" once. It's a quiet decision, over and over again, to not carry bitterness. Caitlin's calm responses and refusal to get dragged into drama show what it means to forgive in real-time—when it's the hardest. She keeps her head down and keeps playing, not just for personal gain, but for the growth of women's basketball and those watching her example. For young athletes, this verse reminds us that Christ's forgiveness fuels our ability to forgive others. You'll face bad calls, unfair treatment, and challenging moments. However, you can choose to stay grounded in kindness and grace and play for a higher purpose.

WEEKLY GAME PLAN

Reflection: *When someone mistreats you during a game, how do you usually respond—with anger, silence, or grace? Explain what it looks like to play with a heart like Jesus—even when you're pushed, provoked, or disrespected?*

_____

_____

_____

Challenge: This week, when someone frustrates or mistreats you on or off the court, choose to respond with grace. Don't react out of emotion, but respond with forgiveness.

THE PRAYER ZONE

God, thank You for forgiving me more times than I can count. Help me reflect that same forgiveness toward others, even when it's hard. Give me the strength to stay composed when I'm wronged, and the humility to extend grace like Jesus. **Amen.**

CHAPTER 12: WITNESS & CHRIST-LIKE CHARACTER

48

CALLED TO BE DIFFERENT

"Do not conform to the pattern of this world, but be transformed by the renewing of your mind."
Romans 12:2

BEYOND THE SCOREBOARD

In a world that celebrates popularity, performance, and personal fame, **Tim Tebow** has always stood out—for all the right reasons. From his days as a Heisman-winning quarterback at the University of Florida to his time in the NFL and now as a sports analyst and ministry leader, Tebow has never let the game change who he was in Christ.

In 2011, he was mocked for kneeling in prayer, yet he kept praying. He was ridiculed for wearing eye black with Bible verses, yet he kept repping his faith. Tebow didn't just talk about being a Christian; he lived it boldly in the face of criticism, spotlight, and pressure. His life screams that being different is a strength, not a weakness. Now, 15 years later, it's very common to see athletes kneel before games and display Bible verses and crosses to show their reverence to the Lord.

Romans 12:2 reminds us that following Christ means refusing to blend in. You won't always be the most liked, praised, or understood—but when you live with godly purpose, you're set apart for impact. Tebow's example teaches young athletes that your walk with God isn't meant to look like everyone else's. It's intended to inspire others to do the same. On your team, in your sport, and in your school—you are called to be different. Not for attention. But for a greater mission. So, lace up, show up, and let your life reflect the difference Jesus has made in you.

WEEKLY GAME PLAN

Reflection: *What are some ways you feel pressured to "fit in" with the crowd in your sport or school? How can standing out for Christ positively influence your teammates and opponents?*

_____

_____

_____

Challenge: This week, identify one way you can boldly live out your faith in your sport. Don't worry about what others think. Don't hide your light—shine it with confidence.

THE PRAYER ZONE

Dear God, thank You for calling me to be different. Help me to stand strong in my faith even when it's hard or unpopular. Please give me the courage to live boldly and lead by example on and off the field. **In Jesus' name, Amen.**

49

UNASHAMED IN UNIFORM

"For I am not ashamed of the gospel, because it is the power of God that brings salvation to everyone who believes..."
Romans 1:16

BEYOND THE SCOREBOARD

While most know **Brock Purdy** as the 49ers' quarterback, what sets him apart is how unashamedly he lives for Christ. Drafted as "Mr. Irrelevant" in 2022, Purdy's rise to NFL stardom wasn't about proving doubters wrong. It was about staying faithful to what he knew was right. In press conferences, interviews, and even postgame huddles, Brock consistently gives glory to God, unapologetically stating that Jesus Christ is the reason he plays with confidence and joy. While others shy away from mentioning faith in the spotlight, Brock stands firm. Whether under pressure in the pocket or facing national criticism, he remains grounded in his identity in Christ. He wears his jersey with humility and boldness, not just representing a football team—but a Savior.

Romans 1:16 reminds us that the Gospel isn't something to be hidden—it's our source of power, purpose, and identity. Being "unashamed" doesn't mean being loud or forceful. It means being honest, steady, and willing to speak up about your faith when the moment comes.

Teen athlete, you may not be on TV, but your uniform matters. Whether it's a practice jersey or game-day gear, wear it as a witness. When you compete, let your sportsmanship, attitude, and words reflect your faith. Like Brock, let your game point to something greater than stats or trophies. Point it to Christ. Let your uniform represent more than a team—let it represent the Kingdom of God.

WEEKLY GAME PLAN

Reflection: *Do your words and actions on and off the field reflect your faith in Christ? When was the last time you had the opportunity to speak about your faith—did you take it or shy away?*

_____

_____

_____

Challenge: Find one way this week to publicly honor God while in uniform—whether that's through a prayer before practice, encouraging a teammate with a Christ-like attitude, or simply wearing your faith boldly. Let your confidence come not from your skill, but from the Savior you represent.

THE PRAYER ZONE

Heavenly Father, thank You for giving me the courage to live unashamed of the Gospel. Please help me to wear my uniform with integrity, boldness, and grace. May every practice, game, and conversation be an opportunity to represent You well. **Amen.**

50

YOUR GAME, HIS WITNESS

"But you will receive power when the Holy Spirit comes on you; and you will be my witnesses... to the ends of the earth."

Acts 1:8

BEYOND THE SCOREBOARD

On the biggest stages of international soccer, **Alyssa Naeher** doesn't just guard the net—she represents her faith. The U.S. Women's National Team goalkeeper is known not only for her clutch saves but for her quiet, unshakable confidence rooted in Christ. She often writes Bible verses on her gloves before matches, a personal reminder that she plays for something far greater than blocking goals: she plays for God's glory. Naeher doesn't shout her faith from the rooftops—but she lives it in every training session, every game, and every decision. She's a walking testimony that you don't have to be loud to lead. Her poise under pressure, her commitment to excellence, and her encouragement toward teammates speak volumes. When the spotlight hits, her character reflects Christ.

Whether in a World Cup final or local scrimmage, you carry the same opportunity as Alyssa to be a witness every time you compete. Being a witness doesn't require a microphone. It just requires consistency, humility, and boldness to live like Jesus when it matters most. God equips us through the Holy Spirit to reflect His love, courage, and grace in how we compete, lead, and respond.

Young athlete, your talent is your stage—but your character is your testimony. Use your game to shine His name. Let your talents, attitude, effort, and humility point others to Christ, without saying a word. Your game might be the moment someone sees Jesus through you.

WEEKLY GAME PLAN

Reflection: *What do your teammates, coaches, and opponents see in your attitude, effort, and reactions during games or practices? If someone didn't know you, could they tell by your actions that you follow Christ?*

_____

_____

_____

Challenge: Focus on how you respond in high-pressure moments—whether it's a tough call, a missed opportunity, or a teammate's mistake. Choose to reflect Christ in your reactions. Let your game be played with integrity, respect, and humility. Before every game or practice, say a quick prayer: *"Let me be Your witness today, Lord."*

THE PRAYER ZONE

Lord, thank You for allowing me to compete. Help me to be a bold witness for You—not just in what I say, but in how I live, play, and treat others. Let my effort, attitude, and actions all point to You. Use my gifts for Your glory. **Amen.**

51

BE A LIGHT ON THE FIELD

"In the same way, let your light shine before others, so that they may see your good works and give glory to your Father who is in heaven."
Matthew 5:16

BEYOND THE SCOREBOARD

When **Russell Wilson** takes the field, faith is never far behind. The Super Bowl-winning quarterback is known for his incredible leadership, elite talent, and clutch performances. But what truly sets Russell apart is how boldly and consistently he lets his light shine for Christ.

From praying with teammates before games to using postgame interviews to give glory to God, Russell sees the field as his mission field. He once said, *"God has me here not for football, but to be a light."* That light shines in how he carries himself—in his sportsmanship, his kindness toward fans, and in his charity work through the Why Not You Foundation, which empowers youth to overcome adversity.

Being a light for Christ doesn't mean being perfect. It means choosing character over comfort, humility over hype, and grace over pride. In a competitive sports world, that's very rare. Russell shows that athletes can shine bright in their faith without dimming their competitive edge.

Teen athlete, every time you step out on the field, court, or track, you have a choice: play for applause or play to reflect the One who gave you the gift. Let your effort, your encouragement, and grace in how you lose reflect the light of Jesus. Because when your light shines for Christ, others take notice.

WEEKLY GAME PLAN

Reflection: *When you compete, do your words and actions reflect the light of Christ? This week, how can you be a positive influence on your teammates, even when things aren't going your way?*

_____

_____

_____

Challenge: Choose one way to be a light on your team. Whether it's encouraging a teammate who's struggling, praying before competition, or showing good sportsmanship after a tough loss—make your character stand out for the right reasons. Let your game point to something greater.

THE PRAYER ZONE

Thank You, God, for allowing me to play and grow through sports. Help me to shine Your light both in how I play, respond to adversity, and how I treat others. **Amen.**

52

LEAVE A LEGACY FOR CHRIST

"One generation commends your works to another; they tell of your mighty acts."

Psalm 145:4

BEYOND THE SCOREBOARD

Just like Stephen Curry, there is an exceptional Christian female athlete who deserves to be recognized more than once in this devotional. She embodies everything that Christ calls us to do in our lives. When people talk about greatness in character, a witness for Christ, and humble in the their sport, one name always rises to the top—**Katie Ledecky.** She's earned the utmost respect through her dominance in the pool, and her Olympic medals shine bright. But what shines even brighter is Katie Ledecky's grace, humility, and faith in Christ that define the legacy she's building outside the pool.

Katie is open about the values that guide her. She credits her Catholic faith as the steady anchor in her life, helping her stay humble through success and resilient through adversity. She attends Mass regularly, prays before competitions, and has said, *"My Catholic faith is very important to me. It always has been, and it always will be."*

Psalm 145:4 reminds us that our legacy isn't just about what we accomplish, but it's who we lead to Christ by the way we live. Katie's legacy is marked by excellence, but even more by her unwavering commitment to represent Christ through her selflessness, discipline, grace, and unbreakable faith. Young athlete, you don't have to win medals to leave a legacy. Whether you're in practice, competition, or the classroom, let your life reflect Jesus so clearly that others see Him through you.

WEEKLY GAME PLAN

Reflection: *What kind of legacy are you building through the way you compete, speak, and treat others? What small actions could you take this week that would leave an eternal impact on your teammates?*

_____

_____

_____

Challenge: Write down how you want others to remember you—not just as an athlete, but as a follower of Christ—and start living it out today.

THE PRAYER ZONE

Father, thank You for allowing me to represent You. Help me remember that my greatest legacy isn't a trophy or title, but the way I reflect Your love to others. Give me the boldness to shine for You in every practice, every game, and every interaction. May my life be a witness for Christ, so others see Him through me. **Amen.**

OUR SINCERE GRATITUDE

Thank you for being a part of this mission to raise up the next generation of faith-driven champions!

If this devotional has helped you grow in faith, rise above challenges, and play with purpose, we'd love your review to help inspire the next rising athlete.

Your review doesn't just help us spread the good news—it helps other athletes find the encouragement, strength, and biblical truth they need to thrive in both sports and life. Please scan the QR code below to leave a review. It only takes a few seconds, and we'd greatly appreciate it!

THE SEASON DOESN'T END HERE

You've made it through the last devotion, but this is far from the finish line. Week by week, you trained your heart, built your faith, and learned how to compete with a higher purpose. This devotional wasn't about checking the boxes or earning a spiritual trophy. It was about your transformation as a Christian athlete and learning that greatness isn't just measured by stats. The way you lead, influence, serve, forgive, persevere, and worship through your sport is what truly sets you apart from other athletes.

You've read stories of athletes who trained hard, failed forward, bounced back, and boldly represented Christ in victory and defeat. Like you, many of them started in small gyms, local pools or parks, and neighborhood teams. They weren't superstars overnight. But what fueled their rise to the top wasn't just talent—it was their unwavering faith and trust in God.

As with sports, one season ends so another can begin. Continue your transformation into the athlete God has planned for you. Open your Bible before you lace up. Say a prayer before each game. Encourage the teammate who's struggling. Compete with integrity when no one's watching. Let your light shine—not just in how you play, but in how you reflect Christ.

Let this devotional be your start—not your finish.

SCRIPTURE SOURCES

Throughout this devotional, Scripture verses have been drawn from multiple Bible translations to bring clarity and impact to each lesson. The following translations were used: New International Version (NIV), English Standard Version (ESV), and New Living Translation (NLT). Each verse has been carefully chosen to communicate biblical truth in a way that resonates with today's rising athletes. Used by permission. All rights reserved.

Biblica, Inc. (2011). *The Holy Bible: New International Version*. (Original work published 1973). Biblica, Inc.

Crossway. (2001). *The Holy Bible: English Standard Version*. Crossway Bibles.

Tyndale House Foundation. (2015). *The Holy Bible: New Living Translation*. (Original work published 1996). Tyndale House Publishers, Inc.

www.ingramcontent.com/pod-product-compliance
Lightning Source LLC
Chambersburg PA
CBHW061650120626
46550CB00003B/894